MARTIN
BUBER

Makers of the Modern Theological Mind

Bob E. Patterson, Editor

Makers of the Modern Theological Mind

Bob E. Patterson, Editor

MARTIN BUBER

by Stephen M. Panko

HENDRICKSON
PUBLISHERS
PEABODY, MASSACHUSETTS 01961-3473

MARTIN BUBER

Copyright © 1976
Hendrickson Publishers, Inc.
P.O. Box 3473
Peabody, Massachusetts 01961–3473
All rights reserved.
Printed in the United States of America

ISBN 0–943575–59–1

Library of Congress Cataloging-in-Publication Data

Panko, Stephen M.
    Martin Buber / by Stephen M. Panko.
        p. cm.
    Reprint. Originally published: Waco, Tex.: Word Books,
c1976. (Makers of the modern theological mind).
    Includes bibliographical references.
    ISBN 0–943575–59–1
    1. Buber, Martin, 1878–1965.   I. Title. II. Series:
Makers of the modern theological mind.
    [B3212.B84P25 1991]
    296.3'.092–dc20
                                                    90–28699
                                                    CIP

To the most magnificent human being I have ever known...
one who knows the meaning of love...
who always understands...
a great lady...
my dearest friend...
my wife...

Jessie

Contents

Editor's Preface

Who are the thinkers that have shaped Christian theology in our time? This series tries to answer that question by providing a reliable guide to the ideas of the men who have significantly charted the theological seas of our century. In the current revival of theology, these books will give a new generation the opportunity to be exposed to significant minds. They are not meant, however, to be a substitute for a careful study of the original works of these makers of the modern theological mind.

This series is not for the lazy. Each major theologian is examined carefully and critically—his life, his theological method, his most germinal ideas, his weaknesses as a thinker, his place in the theological spectrum, and his chief contribution to the climate of theology today. The books are written with the assumption that laymen will read them and enter into the theological dialogue that is so necessary to the church as a whole. At the same time they are carefully enough designed to give assurance to a Ph.D. student in theology preparing for his preliminary exams.

Each author in the series is a professional scholar and theologian in his own right. All are specialists on, and in some cases have studied with, the theologians about whom they write. Welcome to the series.

BOB E. PATTERSON, EDITOR
Baylor University

I. Martin Buber: His Life

He was a short plump man with a bit of a paunch. While almost completely bald, he had a fringe of white hair that met an equally white luxurious growth of moustache and beard that covered the lower portion of his face.

His home was an old Arab house with a red tile roof and a garden in front of it in which grew two tall trees, a cypress and a palm. The street on which he lived—the Lovers of Zion Street—was in a quiet section, green with trees and shrubbery. Before Israel's independence, it had been the quarter of the wealthy Arab merchants. The Arab Christian family who had lived in his house left Jerusalem shortly before the war began in 1948. It was located but a short distance south of Mt. Zion and the old walls of the ancient city.

It was in this peaceful and tranquil environment that Martin Buber spent the last twenty-seven years of his life. They were among the happiest of the eighty-seven that were his.

He loved Israel and it meant a great deal to him to live

in Jerusalem. He lived simply. His bedroom and his study
were on the ground floor of his home. The furniture was old
and dark and heavy. It looked as if he had brought it with
him to Jerusalem from Europe. The house was filled with
books.

Living with him was his granddaughter, Barbara Gold-
schmitt, who served as his housekeeper. His secretary was
frequently there but did not live in the house.

He loved to have visitors and the conversations would go
on endlessly. When someone phoned, the caller would hear
a click and then a quick, sharp one-word response: "Buber."

When he received visitors, Dr. Buber would most often
be in his study in his shirt sleeves, without a tie, and wear-
ing slippers while sitting behind his desk. His eyes were
gray and proud, tender and secure. His fingers were small
and delicate, but his touch was firm. He acted in a courteous,
rather old-fashioned way. When he spoke, it was in a slow,
precise Hebrew with Germanic inflections. His voice was always low and seemed tinged with melancholy. In conversation, he would interlock his fingers and rest them on his
paunch when listening to someone speak. He would then
move his hands to his forehead as he considered his response.
He listened with intense concentration when someone spoke
to him, but he did not like general questions and often would
prompt his questioner with "be specific." He would get angry
with anyone who attempted to ask him questions of a personal
anecdotal nature. He insisted that his personal life was his
own concern and no one else's.

Before his retirement from Hebrew University in Jerusalem in 1951, it was said that some of his lectures on philosophy were reminiscent of the atmosphere that must have been
distinctive of the dialogues of Socrates. On other occasions,

when he was lecturing, he showed an earnestness and a zeal which bordered on the veneration with which Hasidic followers are said to follow the words and teachings of their rabbi.

He disliked anything superficial. What counted most to him was the sincerity and the impulse behind a person's actions. They could often be more meaningful than the person's actions themselves.

In short, he was a simple and a humble man. He tried to be honest with others and he respected their thoughts. He was a scholar who attempted to use all of his vast knowledge to improve the relationships between people. Just a simple, humble, scholarly man . . . yes. But more . . . he was much, much more . . .

* * *

Martin Buber was born in a middle-class Jewish family in Vienna on February 8, 1878. His parents were not especially intellectual or religious. When he was three years old, they were separated, and he went to live with his grandparents in Lvov (Lemberg), then the capital city of Galicia, the crown province of the Austro-Hungarian Empire. His grandparents on his father's side were both people of high rank—noble, in the exact sense of the word.

His grandfather, Solomon Buber, was famous as a Hebrew scholar. He had published several critical editions of the Midrash, a classic Jewish exegesis of the Scriptures. Both Solomon and his wife, Adela, were little inclined to discuss their personal affairs in front of their grandson and never discussed what had taken place between his parents. There was a strong emphasis on Jewish tradition in the home, but along with the study of the Bible and the Talmud, there was an emphasis on European languages. Solomon and Adela Buber were a new kind of learned Jew; they felt as comfortable studying Goethe and Schiller and other German authors as they were with the Torah and the Midrash. Their grandson was exposed to the same mixture of classical Jewish and non-Jewish writings. He did not go to school until he was ten years of age, but was taught privately at home.

His grandparents were a great influence in his life. His grandfather took him for long walks so that he might learn to love nature as well as books. His grandmother ran the family grain business so that her husband would be free to study.

His earliest memory revolved around an incident which occurred when he was three years of age. It made him aware of the fact that life sometimes had its tragic aspect:

> The house in which my grandparents lived had a great rectangular inner courtyard surrounded by a wooden balcony extending to the roof on which one could walk around the building at each floor. Here I stood once in my fourth year with a girl several years older, the daughter of a neighbor, to whose care my grandmother had entrusted me. We both leaned on the railing. I cannot remember that I spoke of my mother to my older comrade. But I hear still how the big girl said to me: "No, she will never come back." I know that I remained silent, but also that I cherished no doubt of the truth of the spoken words. It remained fixed in me; from year to year it cleaved ever more to my heart, but after more than ten years I had begun to perceive it as something that concerned not only me, but all men. Later I once made up the word "Vergegnung" —"mismeeting," or "miscounter"—to designate the failure of a real meeting between men. When after another twenty years I again saw my mother, who had come from a distance to visit me, my wife, and my children, I could not gaze into her still astonishingly beautiful eyes without hearing from somewhere

the word "Vergegnung" as a word spoken to me. I suspect that all that I have learned about genuine meeting in the course of my life had its first origin in that hour on the balcony.[1]

In his grandfather the boy was exposed to a deep, yet enlightened Jewish piety. In later life he wrote of his grandfather: "The spiritual passion which manifested itself in his incessant work was combined with the untouchable, unperturbable childlikeness of a pure, human nature and an elementary Jewish being. . . . He did not trouble himself about Judaism, but it dwelled in him." [2]

While Martin was still very young, Buber's father became interested in farming and assumed the responsibility of managing his parents' farm, which became famous throughout Eastern Galicia because of its progressive methods. The boy often went with his father on visits to the farm and to the peasants who lived on it. He was impressed by the way his father treated the animals. It was as if they were people.

When he was nine years old, he began to spend each of his summers on the family farm. During one of those summers he had an experience which took him a little further down the path that was to lead to his mature philosophy of dialogue.

When I was eleven years of age, spending the summer on my grandparents' estate, I used, as often as I could do it unobserved, to steal into the stable and gently stroke the neck of my darling, a broad dapple-gray horse. It was not a casual delight but a great, certainly friendly, but also deeply stirring happening. If I am to explain it now, beginning from the still very fresh memory of my hand, I must say that what I experienced in touch with the animal was the Other, the immense otherness of the Other, which, however, did not remain strange like the otherness of the ox and the ram, but rather let me draw near and touch it. When I stroked the mighty mane, sometimes marvellously smooth-combed, at other times just as astonish-

ingly wild, and felt the life beneath my hand, it was as though
the element of vitality itself bordered on my skin, something
that was not I, was certainly not akin to me, palpably the
other, not just another, really the Other itself; and yet it let
me approach, confided itself to me, placed itself elementally in
the relation of Thou and Thou with me. The horse, even when
I had not begun by pouring oats for him into the manger, very
gently raised his massive head, ears flicking, then snorted
quietly, as a conspirator gives a signal meant to be recognizable
only by his fellow-conspirator; and I was approved.

But once—I do not know what came over the child, at any
rate it was childlike enough—it struck me about the stroking,
what fun it gave me, and suddenly I became conscious of my
hand. The game went on as before, but something had changed,
it was no longer the same thing. And the next day, after giving
him a rich feed, when I stroked my friend's head he did not
raise his head. A few years later, when I thought back to the
incident, I no longer supposed that the animal had noticed my
defection. But at the time I had considered myself judged.[3]

As he approached his bar mitzvah, despite the orthodox
atmosphere of his grandparents' home, he began to have
doubts about organized Judaism. At his bar mitzvah cere-
mony at the age of thirteen, instead of delivering the usual
presentation on a passage of the Bible, he gave a talk on
Schiller. Shortly thereafter he stopped putting on tefillin,
gave up saying his daily prayers, and no longer observed
most of the other religious practices that he had been following. He did, however, continue to study the Bible and the
Talmud very earnestly.

When he was fourteen his father married again and moved
to Lemberg. Martin left the home of his grandparents and went
to live with his father. While there he entered a Polish gymna-
sium from which he graduated in 1896. He then entered the

University of Vienna when he was seventeen to study philosophy and the history of art. After Vienna, he went to the Universities of Berlin, Leipzig and Zurich. During his student years, Buber's studies had no clear direction. His interests were secular and he took nothing in the way of Jewish studies. He enjoyed the life of the cities where he attended the great universities. In Vienna, he went to the dramas at the *Burgtheater*. He would rush up three flights of stairs to sit in the highest gallery after spending hours standing in wait for tickets. Day after day he would look down far below him to watch the drama unfold when the curtain was raised.

In Leipzig he often went to the Church of St. Thomas where Bach had played and heard Bach's music rendered as Bach himself would have wished. In later years as he thought back on the effect Bach had made on his life, he felt that his life and thinking had been modified in some way by Bach's music. Just how, he was uncertain, since he felt he was unable to delve into such great and mysterious experiences.

It was also in Leipzig in 1900 that he became involved in Zionism, the new doctrine of which Theodor Herzl was the dynamic leader. It gave him a Jewish cause he could believe in. The next year while he was only twenty-three, he became editor of *Die Welt*, the official Zionist journal. One of the writers for *Die Welt* was Paula Winkler, a Roman Catholic, who later became Buber's wife and was converted to Judaism.

Buber, however, soon found himself out of sympathy with Herzl's purely political program. Herzl looked for a national solution for the Jewish people in Palestine, believing that would bring about a renaissance, while Buber was drawn to a minority in the Zionist movement who believed that Zionism must be based on a great cultural renaissance and must direct its efforts to achieving a greater measure of spiritual health and integrity among Jews throughout the world. Buber felt that the renewal of true Jewish existence and spiritual regeneration was more important than a political nationalism which limited itself to achieving a territorial goal.

He became disillusioned with the politics of the Zionist movement. In 1904 he decided to live in solitude and attempted to find a new direction which had a deeper meaning than that which was found in politics. Formal orthodox Judaism had been a disappointment to him. And although Zionism had emphasized the end rather than the means, it brought him back to Judaism and allowed him to reappraise it. He sought for that within Judaism which he felt he could accept intellectually and emotionally. As so often happens in life, he found himself headed in a totally unexpected direction: toward Hasidism. This was a religious movement which developed among Eastern European Jews about the middle of the eighteenth century. The Hasidim are those who are loyal to the covenant, or those who are truly pious. They compose a society of men led by *zaddikim*, "holy" or righteous" men, those who have stood the test, the "proven ones," who have attracted disciples and formed little communities.

Buber's first exposure to Hasidism occurred while he was a boy spending his summers on the family farm in Bukovina. On occasion, his father took him to the nearby town of Sadagora, the seat of a dynasty of *zaddikim*. There he saw the Hasidim swaying and chanting in ecstasy around the man they followed because of his spiritual perfection.

> . . . when I watched the Rabbi stride through the rows of

supplicants, I understood what a leader was; when I saw the hasidim dance with the Torah, the Scroll of the Law, I knew what a community was.[4]

In later life he stated that among the Hasidim in Sadagora he found "the living germ of humanity, true community and true guidance." [5] The world is for the *zaddik*, the perfect and just man. The spirit of man can only be saved by the righteous and just man. He began to feel the impact of Hasidism. The Hebrew word *hesed* means "loving-kindness"; so a Hasid is a man who approaches life and the world with loving-kindness, affirming and hallowing the reality around him and thereby changing it and himself.

But all of this faded into his subconscious as the years passed. His summers as he grew older were spent elsewhere and he began to forget these early Hasidic memories. After a few years he returned to an estate that his father had acquired near Czortkow and there came into contact with another community of Hasidim. This time he had outgrown his childhood perceptions and felt himself intellectually estranged from them. He felt no part of their world and even looked down on them, believing himself to be more rational than they were. Although he was not as affected at this encounter as he had been earlier in Sadagora, he did hear for the first time the name of Rabbi Israel ben Eliezer (1700–1760), who was called Baal Shem-Tov, which literally means "Master of the Good Name" (the name of God). It was Baal Shem-Tov who had founded the Hasidic movement in the villages of Poland in the mid-eighteenth century from whence it spread throughout Eastern Europe.

All this was almost forgotten as Buber went into his years of university life. But in 1904, soon after Herzl's death, he happened to pick up a little book entitled *Zevaat Ribesh*, the teaching and testament of the Baal Shem-Tov. At that moment, he later wrote,

> . . . the words flashed toward me, "He takes unto himself the quality of fervor. He arises from sleep with fervor, for he is hallowed and become another man and is worthy to create and is become like the Holy One, blessed by Him, when He created His world." It was then, that, overpowered in an instant, I experienced the Hasidic soul. The primally Jewish opened to me, flowering the newly conscious expression in the darkness of exile: man's being created in the image of God I grasped as deed, as becoming, as task. And this primally Jewish reality was a primal human reality, the content of human religiousness. Judaism as religiousness, as "piety," as Hasidut, opened to me there. The image of my childhood, the memory of the zaddik and his community, rose upward and illuminated me: I recognized the idea of the perfected man. At the same time I became aware of the summons to proclaim it to the world.[6]

After having this experience Buber decided to withdraw from his active life of writing and lecturing and he spent the next five years in a secluded and intensive study of Hasidic teachings. This study convinced him that Hasidism in its early period, roughly from 1750 to 1825, had produced a surge of creative religious living that was unparalleled in history; a society which lived according to its faith. Its uniqueness lay in the fact that it was not confined to a monastic community which removed itself from the world, but rather it was a living reality seen in ordinary Jewish villages existing among all sorts of people.

Buber's encounter with Hasidism, with its emphasis on joyful worship of God in the everydayness of this world, changed him from being a European intellectual who was searching for meaning in Judaism, into a thinker whose mind and whose most profound allegiance were irrevocably Jewish.

He has spoken of the prophets of Israel as "national-universalists" and this was what he himself became.[7] His whole life expressed a passionate concern for all of humanity, but this concern always arose out of his loyalty to his own people and to their faith.

The result of his five years of concentrated study of Hasidism and Hasidic literature was a lifelong immersion in the life and thought of the Hasid. It transformed him and he saved it from being lost to the world. As Hermann Hesse, the famous Swiss novelist and poet, has written:

> Martin Buber is in my judgment not only one of the few wise men who live on the earth at the present time, he is also a writer of a very high order, and, more than that, he has enriched world literature with a genuine treasure as has no other living author—the Tales of the Hasidim. . . . Martin Buber . . . is the worthiest spiritual representative of Israel, the people that has had to suffer the most of all people in our time.[8]

In a very real sense, it has been Buber's solitary effort that has brought to the Western world a knowledge of a movement which he believed to be the most unique and powerful phenomenon to come out of the Diaspora (the dispersion of the Jews after their exile from Palestine).

The five years he spent in meditation and private study proved to be one of the most rewarding periods of his life. He made an intensive search for all that could be found concerning Hasidic teachings, beliefs, and practices. Most of the tales he discovered had been handed down from one generation to another—usually by word of mouth—from the followers of one great rabbi to the followers of another.

At first Buber had a tendency to emphasize the mystical aspects of Hasidic teaching; the belief that through ecstatic prayer the individual could, at rare moments, become united with God. But as he progressed, the practical side of Hasidism had a greater meaning for him. He came to believe that mysticism was illegitimate because it took religion out of the everyday lives of men and brought into existence a division in man's life. The aim of religion was to "hallow the everyday." When the mystic claimed he could find unity with God, he was under an illusion because the separated self continued to exist.

Mysticism did, however, play a significant role in Buber's early thinking. At the turn of the century there was a revival of mysticism. It was brought about by an interest in Oriental religions and in mythology. It was also a reaction against specialized knowledge and determinism and was part of a continuation of the mystical tendencies of German Romanticism. Buber's early thought was strongly influenced by all these movements, along with Hinduism and Buddhism. Taoism came a bit later, but continued into his mature thought. The German mystics, such as Meister Eckhart and Jacob Boehme, also affected his thinking at this time. In fact, he has referred to the former as "the greatest thinker of Western mysticism." [9]

One of the reasons Buber was drawn to mysticism was its emphasis upon rare moments of ecstasy. He believed that ecstatic experiences allowed one to concentrate life's energies and brought about an outpouring of creative vitality.[10] But with his reading of Kierkegaard, Buber shifted his interest from the mystical aspects of Hasidism to that side of it which emphasized filling everyday life with "the breath of eternity." [11]

His early thinking on mysticism evolved later into existentialism and finally resulted in dialogical philosophy. Although his ideas from each period of his life are in some way incorporated into his evolving philosophy, by the time he published his most famous work, *I and Thou*, in 1923, mysticism was gone from his thought. "The central reality," he wrote, "of the everyday hour on earth, with a streak of sun on a maple twig and the glimpse of the eternal Thou, is greater for us than all enigmatic webs on the brink of being." [12] This was what he found in Hasidism. Not mystical union, but rather joy and wonder at the everyday things of life.

The spirit of Hasidism as understood by Buber is exemplified in a beautiful story entitled "If Not Higher," written by Isaac Loeb Peretz. It seems that on every Day of Atonement the rabbi disappears from the synagogue for a few hours. One of his followers has suspicions that he is secretly meeting with God so he follows him. He sees the rabbi take off his fine clothing and put on coarse peasant clothes. The rabbi then enters the cottage of an invalid woman, cares for her, cleans her room, and prepares her meals. When the follower returns to the synagogue and is asked, "Did the rabbi ascend to heaven?" he replies, "If not higher." [13]

It was this idea of joyful worship of God, of meeting him through acts of love toward one's fellowman, that so spoke to Buber. One afternoon after he had had a morning of "religious enthusiasm," an unknown young man came to visit him. Buber was friendly and attentive and spoke openly with the young man. Not long after, he learned that the young man had died. He then realized that the questions that he had been asked were not casual ones. The young man had not come for a chat, but rather for a decision. He was in despair and needed help. Buber saw that he should have given meaning to the young man's life, not just friendly conversation.

From that moment on, Buber renounced that which was religious per se. He saw the religious as nothing other than an exaltation or an ecstasy. He believed that all he possessed

was the everyday out of which he could never be taken. He
saw that the mystery of life is either not to be disclosed, or
if it is, it is to be found in a man's daily life. He came to
know no fullness but that which existed in every living hour.
He began to feel that life had a claim on him, and although
he believed that he was not equal to it, he nevertheless knew
that he had a responsibility to respond when another spoke
to him and claimed him.

He believed he did not know much more. If that was religion, then he believed that it included everything—everything that is lived, with its possibility for dialogue.[14]

In this one experience Buber was able to indicate his
complete concept of what man's responsibility and his destiny
are in this world. In a very real sense, this is the only insight
that Buber has to offer: man is able to achieve his true humanity—his real place in the world in relation to God—only
in terms of a genuine relationship with others living their
everyday lives. He says it in many ways, and within many
different disciplines, but this is the great truth he brings to
us.

Buber began to collect Hasidic tales in the remote villages
of eastern Poland, and to translate them into German. The
first of the tales that were printed—*The Tales of Rabbi Nachman* (1906)—disappointed him. He had attempted to translate the stories exactly the way he had found them written,
but somehow the message and the purity of the original tales
had been lost as they were retold and handed down from one
generation of disciples to another.

Buber attempted a different approach to translation. Instead of treating the tales literally, he reinterpreted them
through his own being, much like the orchestral conductor who
takes the notes of a great composition and tries to interpret

them in the spirit he believes the composer meant them to be played. Once he began to reproduce the tales as they were told originally, they started to come alive, sometimes as fairy tales, sometimes as parables.

Buber began to feel a union with the spirit of the rabbis who had originally told the tales. He had discovered a way to tell the tales that was more accurate and more closely approximated their original intent than had the versions handed down by the rabbis' disciples.

Other volumes of Hasidic literature began to appear: *The Legend of the Baal-Shem* (1908), *The Great Maggid* (1922), *The Hidden Light* (1924). Slowly over the years he brought out the rich treasure of Hasidic literature which was collected in a volume entitled *Tales of the Hasidim* (1928).

Buber strove to bring to the Western world what he referred to as legendary reality. He believed Hasidism to be the one great effort of the Jews in the Diaspora to try to establish a true and just community on the basis of religious beliefs and principles. But even though two hundred years ago Hasidism rebelled against formal, mechanical worship in the synagogue, it too over the centuries has become ritualized and stagnant. The tales that Buber has preserved, however, are still able to capture the period of its greatest achievement. Without his endeavors the world would not know of the poetic and religious literature that until his coming had belonged to a minor cult in Judaism.

One of the great ironies in Buber's life was that even though he was the greatest interpreter of Hasidism to the modern world, he was never thought of as a Hasid. He rarely attended synagogue and could not accept the prescribed rituals. And so, even though within a short distance of his home in Jerusalem there were many Hasidic meeting places, he would not have been accepted into any of them, nor would he have wanted to be.

Buber's first public appearance after his years of withdrawal and study of Hasidism came in January, 1909. He spoke on Judaism to the Jewish Student Society of Barkochba at Prague University. Among the students listening that day was Franz Kafka. The relationships and contrasts between Buber's thought and Kafka's work would be an interesting study since they are so evident in Kafka's writings.

In 1916, Buber became the editor of *Der Jude*, a magazine he established in order to emphasize the spiritual and cultural aspects of Judaism which he believed were the foundation of the political aspirations of Zionism. He contributed many articles promulgating those views which had earlier led him to break with the purely political wing of Zionism. By 1924, when he resigned from his position as editor, *Der Jude* had become one of the leading periodicals in Germany expressing serious Jewish thought.

In 1923, Buber accepted an appointment to the newly created chair of Jewish History of Religion and Ethics at Frankfort University. His position was unique in Germany at the time; for that matter, there was no similar position anywhere in the world. Later, his responsibilities were enlarged to include the History of Religions, a discipline which had long been one of his major interests.

In the early 1920s a revival of Jewish studies was taking place in Germany. The Jewish theologians Franz Rosenzweig and Ernst Simon, along with Buber, conducted a unique experiment in adult Jewish education in Frankfort. The famous *Freies Jüdisches Lehrhaus* (Free Jewish Academy), established in 1920 by Rosenzweig, exerted a great influence on German Jewish life during that decade. The three men attempted to introduce the key texts of the Jewish tradition to a generation of Jewish adults who had been estranged from their heritage. It would have been senseless to attempt to teach Hebrew or Aramaic to most of the students, so their studies were limited to translations.

It was out of the need to provide a German text of the Old Testament that Rosenzweig and Buber decided to collaborate on a new translation of the Hebrew Bible into German. In this translation, begun in 1925 and generally agreed to be the finest since that of Martin Luther, the two men tried to create a version of the Old Testament which would avoid the stilted language and "holy" tone of previous versions. They also attempted to reflect as accurately as possible the precise meaning, structure, and poetry of the original Hebrew text. Their work has been recognized as a brilliant success.

Rosenzweig died in 1929 during the translation of the chapters in Isaiah dealing with the suffering servant of God. Buber continued the translation alone, completing it in 1961 while living in Jerusalem.

As significant as was his work of translation, of greater significance were his many volumes of biblical interpretation. Buber's deep concern with the Bible caused him to write a number of monographs and books on biblical history and theology while he was doing his translation. These works have established a reputation for him in both Jewish and Christian circles as one of the foremost interpreters of the Bible during the twentieth century.

James Muilenburg, formerly Professor of Old Testament at Union Theological Seminary in New York, believed that Buber, while devoting himself for more than a generation to

a careful study of the Bible, had come into a living encounter
with the ancient Hebrew words as had no other contemporary
scholar. He felt that Buber's extraordinary understanding of
the vitality and power of words came from his understanding
of man as a listening and speaking being and the uniqueness
of human life when it is involved in hearing and speaking.

Muilenburg recognized Buber as the greatest Jewish thinker
of his generation and an authentic exponent and representative
of the Hebrew way of living and thinking. He also saw him,
however, as the foremost Jewish teacher of Christians. Buber,
more than any other Jewish writer, is able to tell the Christian
what the Old Testament is or is not saying and what he ought
to know and see when he reads that great book.[15]

But Buber was more than a great biblical scholar. His
philosophy was thoroughly grounded in his understanding of
biblical faith. One of the lasting contributions to the religious
and philosophical thought of the twentieth century derives
from Buber's perception of the nature of the Hebrew Bible
as a whole and of its major theses.

In 1923, he published his most famous work, *Ich und Du
(I and Thou)*, which has exerted a tremendous influence on
Western thought, both Jewish and Christian. By that time he
had given up all thought regarding an individualistic religious
mysticism and in this short volume expressed what was to be
his mature philosophy of dialogue. The message of the book—
the message at the heart of Buber's teaching—is that "all real
living is meeting." [16] What is of major concern for Buber is
man's whole situation in this world. He (man) is faced with
many different kinds of relationships. They are so complex
that he is often at a loss as to how to confront them. Buber
opens a new door on these relationships in *I and Thou.*

From 1926 until 1930, along with his teaching responsibilities, Buber edited a journal entitled *Die Kreatur*. Other editors were the Catholic theologian Joseph Wittig and the Protestant physician and psychotherapist Viktor von Weisacher. The periodical was devoted to the educational and social problems that were common to the three religious faiths.

When the Nazis came into power in 1933, they closed the doors of all universities and colleges in Germany to Jewish students. Buber was dismissed from his teaching position by the Nazis. From that time until he left Germany in 1938 he continued to live in the little village of Heppenheim on the Bergstrasse. He labored tirelessly to assist and encourage his fellow Jews in Germany. He served as the director of the Central Office for Jewish Adult Education in Germany. New schools had to be established for Jewish students, since they were barred by the Nazis from attending any German schools. He carried on a spiritual war against Nazism.

In his attempts to build up and maintain the spiritual inner resources of the beleaguered Jewish community in Germany, he wrote and spoke fearlessly. In the spring of 1933 he suggested to a representative body of German Jewry that a cultural institute be established for their own people. It was to be a permanent structure and have the Hebrew Bible as the foundation of its existence. Before the year had ended the *Freies Jüdisches Lehrhaus* in Frankfurt was opened again. It had been closed shortly after Rosenzweig's death in 1929. A second *Lehrhaus* was established in Stuttgart.

In May 1934 Buber called for a conference on Jewish education. It was held at Herrlingen, near Ulm, and he gave the opening address. During this period Buber was at the center of educational activities attempting to bring to the

German Jewish people the message of their Bible during their hour of darkness and despair.

Speaking at the Buber Memorial Seminar on Jewish-Arab Understanding at Tel Aviv in 1966, Ernst Simon referred to Buber's activities in those years: "Anyone who did not see Buber then has not seen true civil courage." [17] But it is possible to get an idea of the extent of that "civil courage." Near the end of 1933 Buber gave an address to the students of the three German-Swiss universities entitled "The Question to the Single One." Actually published in Germany in 1936, it dealt with Kierkegaard and it attacked the very life-basis of totalitarianism. As Buber explained later: "The fact that it could be published with impunity is certainly to be explained from its not having been understood by the proper authorities." [18]

In the autumn of 1934, Buber presented another address at the *Lehrhaus* in Frankfurt entitled "The Power of the Spirit." He openly criticized the pagan glorification of the elemental powers of appetite, sex, and the will to power. He spoke of Christianity's attempt to conquer and control these elemental forces. And finally he spoke of Judaism's attempt to hallow and sanctify them and thereby ultimately to transform them. It was his belief that Judaism was "the most striking instance of this third relationship in the history of the Western world." [19] He courageously repeated his presentation at the Berlin Philharmonic knowing that some two hundred SS men were among those in the audience. He threw down the gauntlet by declaring:

> Heathenism glorifies elemental forces as such; they are considered sacred; they are declared holy, but not transformed. . . . This glorification, this divine rank of theirs, cannot be main-

tained because the spirit which has empowered them cannot draw upon inexhaustible depths. . . . In the end, heathenism necessarily breaks apart into spirit alien to the world and world alien to the spirit.

As a contrast to this, he saw that

in the "reality system" of Judaism, the elemental forces are connected with the living faith in a union holy from time immemorial. Thus, blood and soil are hallowed in the promise made to Abraham, because they are bound up with the command to be "a blessing" (Gen. 12:2). "Seed" and "earth" are promised, but only in order that—in the race of man scattered through the confusion of languages and divided into "islands of the nations" (Gen. 10:5)—a new people may "keep the way of the Lord to do righteousness and justice" (Gen. 18:19) in his land, and so begin building humanity.[20]

Needless to say, there was an immediate Nazi reaction. Buber was banned from speaking in public or to closed meetings of Jewish organizations. A Frankfurt Quaker, however, assumed the risk of assisting him to lecture at closed sessions of non-Jewish organizations, which he did repeatedly.

Buber saw Adolph Hitler as a man who had lost the tension between what he is and what he should be. The secret of Hitler's effectiveness came from "his complete and fundamental absence of restraint." He was a man without conscience. Buber compared him with Jacob Frank, a self-proclaimed messiah of the eighteenth century. Both men believed in nothing other than in their own power. But Buber concluded that a man could not have such a belief in himself unless he felt "commissioned and empowered by the absolute." It would not be possible for a man like Hitler to have this sense of self if he did not believe in any absolute. The absence of restraint, however, was accompanied by the ability and readiness to avoid any self-reflection, preventing someone like Hitler from recognizing his own emptiness.[21]

Buber felt that no one was "absolutely" unredeemable and he believed that, if a devil existed, God could and would redeem him. But man would have to share in the work of redemption. When this is considered, then a person must think of the empirical character of his relationship with another. Within that framework, Hitler could not be addressed nor would he be capable of listening to another.

Buber once listened to Hitler on the radio and knew that the voice he heard was capable of annihilating him and countless others, but he was powerless to deal dialogically with "the poor devil in power." He had to respond but not just to the person; rather he had to confront the situation of which the person was a part.[22]

During the years that he lived in Nazi Germany, he agonized over the plight of the Jewish people: from the intense pain at seeing Jewish children leered at and mocked by former friends, classmates, and teachers to the horror at seeing the concentration camps established. But his faith was never destroyed. He saw that what was happening was part of Israel's destiny. He reminded his fellow Jews that "to Israel belongs the grace to ever renew the primordial bond [the Sinai convenant] by which it first came into being, in just such distress." [23]

But echoing the tormented and agonized question of those who survived or knew of the Nazi concentration camps, Buber asked:

> How is a life with God still possible in a time in which there is an Oswiecim? The estrangement has become too cruel, the hiddenness too deep. One can still "believe" in the God who allowed those things to happen, but can one still speak to

Him? Can one still hear His word? Can one still . . . enter at
all into a dialogic relationship with him? . . . Dare we recom-
mend to . . . the Job of the gas chambers: "Call to Him, for
He is kind, for His mercy endureth forever"? [24]

And he answered his own question. For as long as the Jew
is not detached from his origin, he is safe. All things may
happen to him, but they cannot affect him. Although he is not
able to conceal himself in the "covert of [God's] wings,"
because God is hiding himself from him and from the time
in which he lives, he still can know he is safe because he
knows God is only hiding. This is the nature of the Jew's
security in the darkness of this world. The experiences of this
life make "the doubter, doubt, the man of belief, believe."
"During the day," Buber states, "one does not see any stars."
But the stars exist. And so does God. And the Jew is safe.[25]

By 1938 he was completely silenced by the Nazis. The
situation had gotten so bad that the Frankfort *Lehrhaus* was
closed. At that moment in his life a call came to him to go to
Jerusalem. He was faced with a difficult decision. He was
reluctant to leave Germany, and kept delaying his departure.
He wanted to travel to Jerusalem on a tourist's visa rather
than as an immigrant in order to be able to return if he was
ever needed. But in the end, as urgent appeals from Jerusalem
increased, he left to begin a new life at age sixty.

He accepted the position of Professor of Social Philosophy
at Hebrew University. It might seem that at the threshold of
elderly life Buber would have slowed down; that having found
a place of relative safety and comfort he would have let time
drift by. In actual fact, the years when most men would begin
to wind down became the period in his life of greatest intellectual activity.

In 1940, he wrote the Hasidic chronicle *Gog und Magog*

(translated into English as *For the Sake of Heaven*); in 1942 followed, in Hebrew, *The Teaching of the Prophets* (translated as *The Prophetic Faith*); and in 1944 the great *Moses*. The iron fist of Nazism had come down on Buber's people in Europe. Knowing that tragedy in a nation's life can act as a double-edged sword and recognizing that nothing can separate the Jewish people from their sacred history, he wrote:

> From the moment when a national disaster appears inevitable, and especially after it has become a reality, it can, like every great torment, become a productive force from the religious point of view: it begins to suggest new questions and to stress old ones. Dogmatized conceptions are pondered afresh in the light of the events, and the faith relationship that has to stand the test of an utterly changed situation is renewed in a modified form. But the new acting force is nothing less than the force of extreme despair, a despair so elemental that it can have but one of two results. The sapping of the last will of life, or the renewal of the soul.[26]

Soon, other important works followed: *Images of Good and Evil* is Buber's mature and critical interpretation of the Adam myth; *Right and Wrong, an Interpretation of Some Psalms* expresses, among other things, his view on personal survival.

In the years before the Proclamation of Israel as an independent nation in 1948, Buber was very active, along with Henrietta Szold, Judah Leon Magnes, and others, in the Ihud (Union) Association. They advocated greater cooperation between the Arab and Jewish communities in Palestine and their ultimate goal was to see the establishment of a binational Jewish-Arab state. Needless to say, this was a distinctly unpopular position to take in the tension-filled country at the time, especially considering the immovable opposition of the Arabs to any further immigration into the country. Buber and

the others who shared his views were often attacked and
derided. Nevertheless, even though his stand was unacceptable
to many, his deep sincerity and moral passion were respected
by many others.

It was during this period that Buber completed *Two Types
of Faith*, in which he examines the New Testament and
reclaims Jesus for Judaism. At this time the *Tales of the
Hasidim* appeared, as did the anthology of Hasidic sayings,
Ten Rungs.

In 1951, at age seventy-three, Buber retired from Hebrew
University and settled in Jerusalem to complete his translation
of the Hebrew Bible into German, giving it absolute priority
over his other writings.

In 1952, Buber accepted the Hanseatic Goethe Prize at the
University of Hamburg. The following year, he received the
Peace Prize of the German Book Trade—Germany's highest
literary award—in Frankfurt. When he agreed to accept the
Goethe Prize in 1951, he was bitterly criticized, often by the
same groups who had so strenuously disagreed with his views
regarding cooperation with the Arabs. It was felt that he was
being too lenient and too forgiving toward those who had
assisted the Nazis in persecuting the German Jews. When he
traveled to Frankfurt to accept the Peace Prize, the vehemence
against him was especially intense. If his critics had only taken
the few moments required to read the address he delivered
on that occasion, they might have realized the great stature of
the man.

On September 27, 1953 he was in *Paulskirche* in the city
where he and Franz Rosenzweig and Ernst Simon had taught
in the *Lehrhaus*. He had been gone for fifteen years. Asked to
speak, he did so with passion and dignity.

He referred to the fact that a decade before a great many

Germans killed millions of Jews in a "systematically prepared and executed procedure." Viewing the cruelty as incomparable to any previous event in history, and as one who remained alive, he could only share a common humanity with those who took part in what had transpired in a strictly formal sense. He believed that they were no longer a part of humanity, but had placed themselves within a "monstrous inhumanity" of which he was incapable of conceiving. He was not able even to hate them, and it would have been presumptuous for him to forgive them.[27]

He went on to speak of those Germans who were not directly involved with the horrors of the concentration camps.

Speaking first of those who were aware of what was happening and did nothing to oppose it, he said he was acquainted with the weakness of men, but in his heart he could not condemn them for not seeking martyrdom. But there were those who were unaware of what was happening and were unwilling to discover the truth that lay behind the rumors. These men he could also excuse because he knew how anxious one might become when confronted with a truth he could not face. But there were those "who have become as familiar to me by sight, action and voice as if they were friends." He was referring to those who discovered what was happening and refused to obey orders and were either executed or committed suicide. He felt a special intimacy with these men. "Reverence and love for those Germans now fills my heart." [28]

He went on to express a concern for the youth of Germany who had grown up after these events had occurred and who played no part in the great crime against the Jewish people. He saw these young people faced with an inner struggle: the same struggle faced by people everywhere, the "battle of *homo humanus* against *homo contrahumanus.*" The problem of contemporary man, as Buber saw it, is that a man is unable to speak to other men. War results when men can no longer communicate. Communication breaks down when trust does not exist.

When man faces a crisis he will not become involved in conversation to resolve his problems because trust must exist for conversation to take place. And trust does not exist in a crisis. That was the reason he felt that the cold war was overcoming mankind. In every previous period of peace, men spoke to each other, drawing away the poison from their antagonisms, thus avoiding war. Communication—the "living word of human dialogue" as he referred to it—had become lifeless during a period of nonwar. The debates between statesmen were no longer aimed at conversation but rather at a "faceless public." Even when conferences are convened to develop mutual understanding, genuine communication does not take place. What actually occurs is reflective of what is happening universally: men cannot or will not speak directly to each other because they do not trust one another.[29]

Buber ended his address by challenging men to "release speech from its ban!"[30] It was the message of his life. In the final analysis it must be affirmed that Buber's greatest contribution was not his endeavors as a professor either in Germany or Israel. It was not even his writing. His greatest contribution can be seen in the teaching that went out beyond the universities or the colleges into the lives of individual people. He worked and thought and wrote for "that single person," the man in the crowd ready to be seen as an individual, as one who wanted to be released from his selfishness and subjectivism, into the life of trust.

In 1957, *Pointing the Way* was published. This selection of Buber's essays written between the years 1909 and 1954 had as its main emphasis social and political problems, including the cold war. When early in the next year Dag Hammarskjöld, then Secretary-General of the United Nations, came into possession of a copy of this volume, it had a great impact on him; Buber's thinking reinforced his own.

In writing about their relationship, Buber indicates that after he had delivered a series of guest lectures at Princeton University, the Secretary-General wrote to him stating that he had read *Pointing The Way*. "I want to tell you," he wrote, "how strongly I have responded to what you write about our age of distrust and to the background of your observations which I find in your philosophy." [31]

Subsequently, both men met at the United Nations and discovered that they were truly concerned about the same things. The one "who stood in the most exposed position of international responsibility" and the "one who stood in the loneliness of a spiritual tower" were both disturbed by the way the various national representatives at the United Nations spoke past each other "out the windows." Both men hoped that representatives who were faithful to their mission would enter into a genuine dialogue with each other while there was still time. They felt that there were only two possibilities for mankind: the realization that all men had common interests or the destruction of civilization. Destruction could only be averted if men and nations dealt with each other genuinely so that they could work together cooperatively. And this meant much more than simply coexistence. That was not enough. [32]

It was May 1, 1958; their warm and intense first meeting lasted for two hours. They spoke of philosophy and belief; of how men and women everywhere could be brought into true community by mutual trust and dialogue.

A few weeks later Hammarskjöld was scheduled to receive

an honorary doctorate from Cambridge University. In his speech accepting the degree he spoke of the mistrust that existed among men. His address was entitled "The Walls of Distrust" and in it he quoted from an address given by Buber at Carnegie Hall in New York at the conclusion of his lecture tour in the United States.[33] He quoted so extensively, in fact, that he felt the need to explain why.

> I have done so because out of the depths of his feelings Martin Buber has found expressions which it would be vain for me to try to improve.[34]

In September 1958 and in January 1959 Hammarskjöld was in Jerusalem, and on both occasions he visited Buber at his home. "In the center of our conversation," Buber wrote of the latter meeting, "stood the problem that has ever again laid claim to me in the course of my life: the failure of the spiritual man in his historical undertakings. I illustrated it by one of the highest of the examples that have become known to us: the abortive attempt of Plato to establish his just state in Sicily." [35]

Hammarskjöld was a mystic who was constantly faced with trying to resolve the most complex of political problems, but his beliefs swung very close to those of Buber: "In our age, the road to holiness necessarily passes through the world of action." [36] These words could have been spoken by the Hasidim, but they were spoken by Hammarskjöld and joined together in a spiritual bond the international diplomat and the quiet scholar.

Buber found Hammarskjöld to be warm and understanding in his relationship with him; he was a man who read the works of Meister Eckhart, the medieval German mystic, and the Psalms of the Old Testament.

After the January 1959 visit with Buber, Hammarskjöld never had the opportunity to meet with Buber again, but his thinking was affected by Buber's, right up to his untimely death on September 17, 1961.

Returning to New York from Jerusalem, Hammarskjöld stated at a news conference that when he had time he would like to translate three or four essays from *Pointing the Way* into Swedish. Although there were a few small differences in their thinking, on many points Hammarskjöld said that he and Buber agreed. He felt that Buber had made a major contribution and he wanted to make it more broadly known.[37] Buber was pleased with his suggestion.

In June 1959, Hammarskjöld wrote to the Nobel Prize Committee in Sweden recommending Buber for the Nobel Prize in peace. The fifteen-hundred-word statement expressed admiringly the Secretary-General's high regard for Buber's writing, his thought and his concern for international affairs. His statement was a positive one until the conclusion, when he sounded a negative, equivocal note by referring to the objections that could be offered for not awarding Buber the prize: he was eighty years old, with his life's work behind him, and his achievements were not directly covered by the Nobel Prizes. Hammarskjöld wrote that Buber should perhaps be recognized as the great interpreter of an important culture, who, as one of its sons, had grown to symbolize it. He recommended the Peace Prize, even though his words might indicate that Buber should be given the prize for literature. He hesitated "to see him rewarded" with the latter.[38]

Hammarskjöld's recommendation received support from a number of distinguished persons and it was forwarded to the Norwegian Parliament for consideration. The fact that Buber was an Israeli proved to be a problem that could not be resolved. Those responsible for awarding the Peace Prize felt that it would be unwise to award it to either a Jew or an Arab. The tension in the Middle East made it imperative that should it be awarded to anyone in that area of the world, the prize should be shared jointly. No one of comparable stature to Buber could be found in the Arab world who was advocating peace to the same extent, so Buber's nomination was no longer considered. In 1959, the Nobel Peace Prize was presented to Philip Noel-Baker, the British writer, who advocated disarmament and worked continuously for world peace.

Buber was extremely disappointed. It was his last opportunity to receive one of the world's most prestigious and coveted honors. Ten years earlier he had been nominated for the Nobel Prize in literature by its winner in 1946, Hermann Hesse, the Swiss novelist and poet. At that time Hesse emphasized Buber's wisdom, his great ability as a writer, and his contribution to the enrichment of world literature by his interpretation of the beliefs and the tales to be found in the Hasidic tradition.

It seemed unfair that the reasons for not awarding the Peace Prize to Buber were strictly political. When the award could have encouraged those who believed as he did that a way to peace with the Arabs could be found, the opportunity evaporated.

But there were other awards to take away the disappointment: the Bialik Prize for literature, the most important award of its kind in Israel, and the Erasmus Prize for his contributions to European culture, to name two of the most significant.

There was a lapse of two years during which Buber and Hammarskjöld were not in touch with each other. Then, on August 17, 1961, Hammarskjöld wrote to Buber that he had

been reading some of Buber's works which he had not seen
before and this prompted him to write. He expressed the
thought that he was still interested in translating some of his
writing, but he felt with the "nuances" of Buber's German,
he would only be able to translate "a modest part of its
overtones."

Buber was very pleased that he had heard from Hammarskjöld and that the relationship between them was reestab-
lished. He responded immediately in handwriting on August
23, the only occasion in which Buber wrote to Hammarskjöld, suggesting that even though it was the most difficult of
his works to understand, *I and Thou* was the book which would
best introduce the reader to the concept of dialogue.

Hammarskjöld responded on August 26 accepting the suggestion. The Swedish publishers whom Hammarskjöld
approached with the proposal of translating *I and Thou* were
enthusiastic about it, and he decided to begin work on the
project. He left New York for Africa on September 12. He
took two books with him: Thomas à Kempis's *Imitation of
Christ* and *I and Thou* (in its original *Ich und Du*). While in
Leopoldville in the Congo attempting to resolve a civil war,
he apparently worked on the translation. On September 17
he flew to Northern Rhodesia, leaving behind in his room, to
which he expected to return after his trip, the first twelve
pages of his translation of *I and Thou*. He had made some
handwritten corrections on the first page.

His plane never reached its destination. It crashed in the
jungle, killing everyone aboard.

Buber learned of Hammarskjöld's death over Jerusalem
radio. An hour later he received a letter that had been written
by Hammarskjöld in New York on September 12 advising him
that the publishers in Sweden were pleased with the proposal

to translate *I and Thou*. He indicated that it was his intention
to begin work immediately.

On February 8, 1963, Martin Buber reached the venerable
age of eighty-five. He was still in good health and optimistic
and cheerful. He was pleased by the many young people who
were coming to visit him in his little house on Lovers of Zion
Street, and in July of that year he traveled to Amsterdam to
receive the Erasmus Prize, given to those who have contributed
to the spiritual unity of Europe.

All went well until April 1965 when Buber slipped in his
bedroom and broke his leg. He was taken to the hospital and
operated on. After a month's recuperation he returned to his
home and was confined to bed. He was weak and began to
lose consciousness periodically. It became evident that the end
was near. On Sunday, June 13, 1965, at 10:45 in the morning,
he passed away. His son, daughter, grandchildren, and eight
great-grandchildren were at his bedside when he died.

The President of Israel came to pay his respects, as did the
President of Hebrew University and many of his former
colleagues and students.

The funeral took place the next day, Monday, June 14.
The body lay in state on the Hebrew University campus before
the burial at the Hill of Rest in Jerusalem in a section of the
cemetery set aside for former professors of the university. On
his tombstone is a phrase from the 73rd Psalm—"I am continually with thee."

A few weeks before he died, his family found among his
papers a short handwritten poem in German. It seemed to be
his farewell to this life. It was entitled "The Fiddler":

> Here on the world's edge at this hour I have
> Wondrously settled my life.
> Behind me is a boundless circle

The All is silent, only that fiddler fiddles.
Dark one, already I stand in covenant with you,
Ready to learn from your tones
Wherein I became guilty without knowing it.
Let me feel, let there be revealed
To this whole soul each wound
That I have incorrigibly inflected and remained in illusion.
Do not stop, holy player, before then! [39]

Buber could face and accept his own death. All was "silent" and he was "wondrously settled." Perhaps it would be best to end this sketch of his life by quoting from the editorial published by the *New York Times* shortly after his death.

Martin Buber was the foremost Jewish religious thinker of our time and one of the world's most influential philosophers. . . .

Because Martin Buber lived, there is more love in the world than there would have been without him. And for him that was the reason above all others for the gift of life.[40]

II. I and Thou

It must be acknowledged that Martin Buber was truly one of the greatest thinkers of the modern era. What he thought has affected the thinking and actions of countless others from theologians and philosophers to those in the workaday world who have never heard his name. He was a many-faceted man whose studies carried him into the fields of psychology, sociology, biblical criticism, and education, as well as philosophy and theology. His translation of the Scriptures is recognized as brilliant, reflecting in the German the beauty and the vitality of the original Hebrew text. He is seen as the man who saved the Hasidic tradition and worked to preserve its great stories. He was a champion of the Jewish cause in a time when the tendency among Jewish thinkers was toward assimilation and the presentation of Judaism as broadly humanistic. But his greatest contribution, and that for which he will be remembered the longest, is in the area of anthropology, for it is by understanding his deep concern for man that he himself may be understood. In a world where man is seen as selfish and self-centered, alone and alienated from other men as well as from God, Buber proclaimed that it is possible for man to turn to other men and in genuine relationship with them achieve authentic human existence. His is a "philosophy of dialogue" where human beings come face to face in real life. "All real living is meeting" [1] must be seen as the heart of Buber's thought.

To understand that thought, one must apprehend the fact that his thinking is not intended to affect only man's intellectual life. It does that, of course, but it goes beyond and leads us to an understanding and a deepening of every aspect of human experience, whether it be intellectual, spiritual, psychological, or physical. He directs his attention to concrete questions as opposed to purely philosophical ones: "Why am I here on this earth?" "Why was I created?" "Where am I going?" Buber feels that it is only when we come to grips with questions such as these, questions involving the whole person, that we are asking the important questions in life. But these questions cannot be answered simply by man's intellect alone, since they are real questions arising out of a man's self-awareness.

A study of philosophy through the ages would easily reveal that there are no final answers to these kinds of questions, but asking them is a very necessary part of being alive and human. Reflecting on them is finally the major task of philosophy. But philosophy can becloud the questions and by its language and methods of thought it may even obscure the answers. Buber believes that questions which deal with the nature of man and with his destiny must also deal with concrete situations. Nothing is of any relevance in his thought unless it considers the actual experiences of life.

In Buber's "philosophy of dialogue" we find the most significant aspect of his work. This is clearly seen in *I and Thou* where he speaks of the possibility of genuine conversation between men as they confront each other in their daily activities. Buber's idea of dialogue suggests that men can relate not only to other men in a genuine relatedness but also to the world and to a God involved with the world.

At the very beginning of *I and Thou* Buber indicates that man faces the world with a "twofold attitude." The word *attitude* is not simply a psychological approach to life; it is much more basic. It has to do with a person's confrontation of the world and all the objects and beings in it. It is a fundamental response of the entire self. It goes beyond simply the intellectual or the emotional and involves the whole man. Buber indicates that the "twofold attitude" may be expressed by the primary words I-Thou and I-It. These primary words, especially I-Thou, have an impact on many people today, especially the young in our society who have emblazoned them on banners during demonstrations or on posters in their various living quarters. But often the words are misunderstood and misused. They do not, in themselves, convey their true meaning. They can only be understood when we take the time to study Buber's thinking and recognize the meaning he has given to them.

In a very simple way we may see the difference between the I-Thou and the I-It by realizing that while both deal with existential experience, the former is involved in a genuine engagement while the latter is detached, objective, and removed. Many of Buber's readers tend to believe that the I-Thou attitude is only appropriate to man's relationship with other men, while the I-It attitude is only possible with things. But the meaning of the terms goes beyond any such clear-cut distinction. I-Thou does deal primarily with a person's relationship to other persons, and I-It does deal primarily with one's relations to things, but it must be understood that either attitude may develop toward anything or anyone.

Buber sees three facets to life: that which we experience when we live with other men; that which we confront in nature; and the life we experience when dealing with "spiritual existences." By this last term Buber does not mean extrasensory beings or experiences, but rather those things that have been brought into being by human creativity, such as great works of art, or music, or even systems of thought. The Thou may be present in our relations with all three facets of life, and when it is, only then do we experience real life. It is only when man meets the Thou, the other, that he really becomes himself, an I.

On the level of I-Thou, the deepest meanings of existence are disclosed; man becomes involved with other men or with the things around him as a person to a person, as a subject to a subject. "Meeting" or "encounter" takes place mutually. "The primary word I-Thou can only be spoken with the whole being." [2] And the whole being addresses another with directness, intensity, and presentness. When an I meets a Thou, fate and causality no longer play a role. These come from a world of order. The meeting of the I with a Thou goes beyond this. The I-Thou relation permeates the world of the It—the world of objects and things—and is not affected by it, since the meeting of I and Thou is beyond time and space; it is the real, filled present. It is a present of wholeness and intensity. But it is not an inner experience; it exists only because meeting and relation are taking place.

The I-It relation, on the other hand, is an attitude of detachment. It examines rather than experiences, as does the I-Thou relation.

> The I of the primary word I-It . . . has no present, only the past. Put in another way, insofar as man rests satisfied with the things that he experiences and uses, he lives in the past, and his moment has no present content. He has nothing but objects. But objects subsist in time that has been.[3]

The I-It finds no meaning in the present, as does the I-Thou. It experiences the present only as a means to reach some end. I-It knows others—be they human or things—only as objects. They have no uniqueness in themselves except as they relate to other objects and can be used.

When the I experiences an It, this is planned and with a purpose. The I in an I-It relation does not go outside of himself to confront the It, and the It does not respond, but just allows itself to be experienced. The Thou, however, comes through grace and cannot be planned for. Yet when the Thou is experienced, the I must go outside of himself to do so, for there must be a direct relation, and the Thou responds to the meeting. This kind of relation can only exist when the I speaks with its whole being, but a whole being exists only when the I is able to speak the Thou.

> The primary word I-Thou can be spoken only with the whole being. Concentration and fusion into the whole being can never take place through any agency, nor can it ever take place without me. I become through my relation to the Thou; as I become I, I say Thou.[4]

The I-It attitude is often assumed by the scientist as he attempts to maintain an objective view of that which he is studying without any involvement on his part. The same I-It attitude may also be applied by the social scientist as he observes the behavior of other men, never himself becoming involved with them either. The I of the I-It attitude never

engages that with which it deals but always stands back. The
I of the I-Thou relation finds itself deeply involved, recognizing in the other an affirmation of itself.

Perhaps the best way to understand what Buber is saying
is to use an illustration dealing with the third facet of life:
man's relationship with "spiritual existences," or in this instance, more specifically, music. Let us imagine that you
have been presented a ticket to listen to a nationally known
pianist. You look forward to the performance, knowing that
an evening of fine music is one of your most rewarding and
satisfying experiences. When the performer comes on the
stage you find yourself filled with excitement. He begins to
play, but nothing happens to you. Although his technique is
superb, for some unknown reason you find yourself thinking
about it and not the music. You think about his dexterity, his
ability to play difficult passages. Then you find yourself comparing him with other pianists you have heard and you begin to
formulate in your thoughts a critique of the performance
that you plan to share with friends later that evening. In
short, you have an I-It experience. You do not become involved with the music or the pianist. You stand back and
observe all that is happening with a detached attitude. It does
not in any way affect you, the real you, deep inside.

Let us compare that evening with another. You are again
given a ticket to attend the concert of another pianist, but
one you hardly know. You are not feeling well. You have
had a hard day and are exhausted, even a little depressed.
You would prefer not to attend the concert, but you do not
wish to injure the feelings of the friend who has given you
the ticket. And so you go prepared to waste an evening. But
something happens. From the moment the performer begins
to play, you lose all thought of everything but the music.

You are involved in the deepest sense. You do not think
about technique, or making comparisons, or developing a
critique; you think and feel and experience only the music.
It is as if the soul of the composer and the soul of the pianist
are speaking directly to your soul. You respond with your
entire being; not just intellectually or even just emotionally,
but completely, with your whole self. Feelings of depression
and tiredness are all gone. All that exists is the moment, but
it is not a moment in time. It is the present, but it goes beyond
time since you are lost in it completely. In this experience
you are meeting the Thou, for Buber tells us that the Thou
is met with spontaneity. Should you, in the midst of the encounter, become conscious of what is happening; should you
become aware of listening and enjoying a great moment, the
Thou would disappear instantly, for then you would no longer
be involved, you would be detached and an objective observer.

And yet all great evenings must end, and all meetings with
the Thou must become a meeting with an It. Every Thou,
Buber feels, must become an It. That is "the exalted melancholy of our fate," [5] he states. Most of our experiences in life
are in the realm of I-It. Although the chief emphasis of
Buber's *I and Thou* is to show that human existence must be
seen as of a personal nature, with all that this implies, no man
can live continually in the presence of the Thou. The Thou
is always here and now, and man, Buber tells us, cannot "live
in the bare present." It is only in the past that life can be
organized. And the past is always in the realm of the It.

> In all the seriousness of truth, hear this: without It man can-
> not live. But he who lives with It Alone is not a man.[6]

So both the It and the Thou are necessary to man's life, and
while the It helps a man to develop perspective, the Thou

causes him to experience life on its deepest and most meaningful level. Of course, this must mean, in most instances,
man's relations with other men, for it is in human confrontation and involvement with other human beings that the Thou
is most readily encountered.

Buber feels that the I-Thou relationship is experienced best
when love exists between a man and a woman, especially a
husband and wife. It is when a man and a woman live together that they are able to reveal the Thou to each other.
When two people are in love they are able to recognize the
uniqueness that each has, and in marriage two people have
the opportunity to develop an intimacy that is not possible
outside of marriage. Many believe today that love is having
a certain feeling toward another person. As long as that
feeling exists, love exists. When it is gone, love is gone. But
Buber says, "Love is responsibility of an I for a Thou." [7] The
heart of a love relationship is not feeling. A meaningful marriage cannot be based on feeling alone. Feelings are important
to a relationship, but if real love is to exist it must go beyond
feelings.

> Feelings accompany the . . . metaphysical fact of love, but
> they do not constitute it. The accompanying feelings can be
> of greatly differing kinds. The feeling, of Jesus for the
> demoniac differs from his feeling for the beloved disciple:
> but the love is the one love. Feelings are "entertained": love
> comes to pass. Feelings dwell in man; but man dwells in his
> love. . . . Love does not cling to the I in such a way as to
> have the Thou only for its "context," its object; but love is
> between I and Thou.[8]

Love cannot exist without the I-Thou relationship existing
between two human beings, but the I-Thou relationship is
not to be mistaken for love. Buber goes on to state that

you speak of love as though it were the only relation between men. But properly speaking, can you take it even only as an example, since there is such a thing as hate?

So long as love is "blind," that is, so long as it does not see a whole being, it is not truly under the sway of the primary word of relation. Hate is by nature blind. Only a part of a being can be hated. He who sees a whole being and is compelled to reject it is no longer in the kingdom of hate, but is in that of human restriction of the power to say Thou. . . .

Yet the man who straightforwardly hates is nearer to relation than the man without hate and love.[9]

In our world today indifference seems to be a part of our lives. And it is this indifference which destroys the possibility of meeting the Thou in another person. Hatred of another person is not as destructive to relation as is indifference. In order to hate we must, at least, recognize that another person exists. Indifference does not. Take, for example, the man who gets into a taxicab and becomes annoyed at the driver. As minimal as this is in regard to relation, it does recognize that the driver exists. To ride in a cab, pay your fare, and be indifferent to the driver destroys his humanity in your relationship to him.

Many seem to think that the life of dialogue is limited to special occasions or unique experiences and relationships, but this is not so. The life of dialogue is to be found in the life of everyday living and in everyday relationships, whether they be in the home, the office, or the factory. There is no one who is excluded from the possibility of an I-Thou relationship. No special intuition, training, or mystical nature is required.

And so it is that man can relate in a meaningful I-Thou relationship on every level of life and with all things, whether they be human or nonhuman, such as nature and the arts.

There are those who are critical of the possibility of having an I-Thou relationship with inanimate things, because they feel that the I-Thou relationship is strongly personal and can only be shared with those who have a consciousness, and inanimate things do not have a consciousness to the best of our knowledge. But Buber persists in using so personal a term as I-Thou when speaking of man's relationships to inanimate things and works of art. The I-Thou relationship may occur whenever we confront anything that relates to our whole being; whenever detachment from the object disappears, and the other addresses us as an exclusive center of attention, independent of any experiences within ourselves.

It is only in the area of the I-It that we are able to examine all things critically and verify or disprove what we have discovered. In the realm of the I-Thou we are not able to examine objectively and verify or disprove what we have experienced. Whenever we attempt to do so we leave the I-Thou moment and become a part of the detached I-It. On this level we cannot explain the meaning discovered in the I-Thou relation.

Buber has often been criticized because he has been unable to develop a means of examining an authentic I-Thou experience and differentiating it from a false one. Any experience, the critics state, may be considered an I-Thou one if a person chooses. The experience of a murderer with his victim might be seen as an I-Thou relationship by the murderer. How can it be determined that it is not?

Buber would reply that there can never be any objective means whereby universal standards of judgment regarding basic human relationships may be established. This is due primarily to the fact that there is no way to force men to think about the fundamental issues of life in the same way.

The only basis Buber uses to identify the validity of an I-Thou relationship comes out of the richness of the meeting itself.

There is no way for Buber to prove that this is a correct method of judging the validity of one's response to the funda-mental experiences of life, because it is impossible for us to rise above our experiences of relationship and view them from a more just perspective. Truth for Buber comes as a result of experiencing life and not from any intellectual solution to problems. There is a great risk when a person becomes in-volved in political, religious, and social questions, because there is no guarantee that the position that is taken is the truth. He cannot accept any absolute standards of truth and falsity, or right and wrong. Anyone who attempts to estab-lish such absolute standards, whether it be within the church, or a political party, or in a social organization, is involved in a worthless endeavor. Although absolutes promise security, they finally result in either a fanatical devotion to the abso-lutes themselves, which are seen as expressing the ultimate truth, or to pessimistic disillusionment.

> I do not accept any absolute formulas for living. . . . No preconceived code can see ahead to everything that can happen in a man's life. As we live, we grow, and our beliefs change. They must change. So I think we live with this constant dis-covery. We should be open to this adventure in heightened awareness of living. We should stake our whole existence on our willingness to explore and experience.[10]

Instead of absolutism, Buber writes that he has occasionally described his standpoint to his friends as the "narrow ridge."

> I wanted by this to express that I did not rest on the broad upland of a system that includes a series of sure statements about the absolute, but on a narrow rocky ridge between the

gulfs where there is no sureness of expressible knowledge but the certainty of meeting what remains, undisclosed.[11]

Buber does not offer man reassurance. Any security offered by philosophical, social, psychological, moral, or even religious thinkers, or institutions, is repugnant to him. He offers instead a "holy insecurity."

> O you secure and safe ones, he exclaims, you who hide yourselves behind the ramparts of the law (or of theology, or of ethics) so that you will not have to look into God's abyss! Yes, you have secure ground under your feet, while we hang suspended looking out over the endless deeps. But we would not exchange our dizzy insecurity and poverty for your security and abundance. . . . Of God's will we know only the eternal; the temporal we must command for ourselves, ourselves imprint his wordless bidding ever anew on the stuff of reality. . . . In genuine life between men, the new world will reveal itself to us. First, we must act; then we shall receive—from out of our own deed.[12] Woe to the man so possessed that he thinks he possesses God! [13]

The concept of the "narrow ridge" that explains Buber's idea of how a man should face life was explained by him in greater detail when he once said:

> The narrow ridge is the place where I and Thou meet . . . you can think of the narrow ridge as a region within yourself where you cannot be touched. Because there you have found yourself: and so you are not vulnerable.
>
> I have already said that every Thou in our life is doomed to become an It, a thing. The man or woman whom we love, whom we seek to fulfill totally, becomes a given imperfect person with a known nature and quality. A young medical student dreams passionately of curing suffering humanity. Then he becomes a doctor in a crowded hospital, with pressure, with not enough time to devote to every patient. And the suffering humans become objects. They recede to the world of the It. This is

the tragedy of being human. And in order to avoid losing the I-Thou we must make our stand on the narrow ridge, as a company of soldiers takes up its position on an embattled hill and says, "From here we shall not retreat." . . .

The narrow ridge is the meeting place of the We. This is where man can meet man in community. And only men who are capable of truly saying "Thou" to one another can truly say "We" with one another. If each guards the narrow ridge within himself and keeps it intact, this meeting can take place.[14]

One must take a stand on the "narrow ridge" believing in the existence of an absolute while at the same time denying that man can in any way fully express the nature of this absolute. We are able to discover the meaning of life and human existence when we encounter the I-Thou but there is no way that the truth discovered in the encounter can be presented objectively. The "narrow ridge" exists between the approach to life where it is held that it is possible to know the truth and prove it objectively in various propositions and the approach that denies that the absolute exists and all truth is a matter of taste and subjective feelings.

And if one still asks if one may be certain of finding what is right on this steep path, once again the answer is No; there is no certainty. There is only a chance; but there is no other. The risk does not insure the truth for us; but it, and it alone, leads us to where the breath of truth is to be felt.[15]

III. The Eternal Thou

One of Buber's major concerns in life was with God—the eternal Thou, as he referred to him. More specifically he attempted to discover "the close connexion of the relation to God with the relation to one's fellow man."[1] He believed that every finite Thou that is met in life is "a glimpse through to the eternal Thou." Although every finite Thou must become an It, the eternal Thou, by its nature cannot become an It.[2]

How we speak of God is unimportant, Buber says. Many believe that the word *God* itself should be discarded because it has been so misused over the centuries. Although Buber believes that meeting God is more important than how he is addressed, in his work *Eclipse of God* he recounts an incident worth repeating because it shows how much the word means to him.

It seems that at one time Buber was in the house of a "noble old thinker." One morning he arose early to read the galley proofs of the preface of a book he was writing. Since it was a statement of faith, he wanted to review it before it was printed.

Upon entering the study, he found his elderly host already at his writing desk. When he asked Buber what he was carrying and Buber told him, he wanted it read aloud to him. When Buber had done so, the old man was amazed that Buber used the word "God" as often as he did. He felt that the name of God was intended by Buber to be something above all human comprehension, but by speaking about it he believed Buber had "lowered it to human conceptualization"; that to hear the word "God" used the way men use it was almost blasphemous.

There seemed to be an acceptance and an understanding between the two men as they sat and faced each other silently. And then Buber spoke, noting that no other word had been "so soiled" or "so mutilated." It was because of that that he did not give up use of it.

> Generations of men have laid the burden of their anxious lives upon this word and weighted it to the ground; it lies in the dust and bears their whole burden. The races of men with their religious factions have torn the word to pieces; they have killed for it and died for it, and it bears their fingermarks and their blood. Where might I find a word like it to describe the highest? If I took the purest, most sparkling concept from the inner treasure-chamber of the philosophers, I could only capture thereby an unbinding product of thought. I could not capture the presence of Him Whom the generations of men have honored and degraded with their awesome living and dying. I do indeed mean Him Whom the hell-tormented and heaven-storming generations of men mean. Certainly, they draw caricatures and write "God" underneath; they murder one another and say "in God's name." But when all madness and delusion fall to dust, when they stand over against Him in the loneliest darkness and no longer say "He, He" but rather shout "Thou, Thou," all of them the one word, and when they add

"God," is it not the real God Whom they all implore, the One Living God, the God of the children of Men? It is not He Who hears them? And just for this reason is not the word "God" the word of appeal, the word which has become a name, consecrated in all human tongues for all times? We must esteem those who interdict it because they rebel against the injustice and wrong which are so readily referred to "God" for authorization. But we may not give up. How understandable it is that some suggest we should remain silent about the "last things" for a time in order that misused words may be redeemed thus. We cannot cleanse the word "God" and we cannot make it whole; but defiled and mutilated as it is, we can raise it from the ground and set it over an hour of great care.

The old man stood up and walked over to Buber and placed his hand on Buber's shoulder. "Let us be friends," he said. The conversation was over. They had been together, despite their difference of opinion, in the presence of God.[3]

It is man who must go out to meet God, by an act of will. How God meets us and extends to us his grace is not our concern. It is God's. Grace is our concern only when we go out to it and persist in its presence. But in order to meet the eternal Thou a man must become a whole being, which means that he is fully able to accept the present. He does not have to make any preparations or follow any specific practices or meditation because none of these have anything to do with the primal, simple fact of meeting. The barrier of separation must be destroyed and that is accomplished when a man gives up the instinct to possess things. Of course, the acceptance of the present and the destruction of separateness means that a man has already overcome the hold that the world of things has on him. He is not expected to give up the I, as many mystical writings suppose, but rather the I must have already met finite Thou in everyday relationships. Then it is able to meet the eternal Thou.

Whoever enters into a relationship with the eternal Thou no longer sees anything in isolation, because all things and beings are gathered up in the relationship. Everything is seen in the Thou and the world is established on its true basis. To look away from the world or to view it objectively does not help a man to reach God. To see the world in God; to recognize that all things are a part of him and he a part of all things; that is to find him who cannot be sought.[4]

> Of course God is the "wholly Other"; but He is also the wholly Same, the wholly Present. Of course He is the Mysterium Tremendum that appears and overthrows; but He is also the mystery of the self-evident, nearer to me than any I.
> If you explore the life of things and of conditioned being you come to the unfathomable, if you deny the life of things and of conditioned being you stand before nothingness, if you hallow this life you meet the living God.[5]

Many have said that God can be inferred from things—in nature, say, as its author, or in history as its master—but Buber does not agree. He feels that God is that Being who is over against us in the most near, direct, and lasting way. He can only be addressed, not expressed.

Men wish to believe that when they meet God they experience a certain feeling, that feeling is the real element in the relationship. But this is not so. While feelings are important, they are, however, only an accompaniment to the fact of meeting. A relationship with God is truly experienced only by the soul and in a bipolar way. A relation with God is only known as a *coincidentia oppositorum*, a coincidence of oppositions of feeling. In a pure relationship with God you will feel yourself to be simply dependent and simply free. The feeling of dependency is unlike any other you have ever felt; the feeling of freedom is also unique. You feel your-

self to be creaturely and creative. And although dependency
limits freedom and vice versa, in actual fact you experience
both feelings in a limitless way and together at the same time.

But Buber believes that God needs man as well as man
needs God. He writes that within his heart a man knows that
he needs God, but does he realize that God needs him? What
would a man be like if God did not need him? A man needs
God in order to be, and God needs man for the very meaning
of man's life. Poets and others attempt to say more, and often
say too much, about the "God who becomes," but man, in
his heart, knows that "there is a becoming of the God that is."
The world is divine destiny, not divine sport. There is divine
meaning in human life and in the world.

Buber sees prayer and sacrifice as two great servants of
man. The man who prays comes to God in unrestrained dependence and knows that in some incomprehensible way he
has an effect on God—even more so, when he prays without
desiring anything for himself. The man of former times who
presents to God a sacrifice knows—"in a foolish but powerful
way"—that he can and ought to give to God.

Prayer and sacrifice are different from magic, because
magic effects its tricks in a void without entering into relation.
Prayer and sacrifice, however, are set before God and antici-
pate mutual action: "They speak the Thou, and then they
hear." [6]

Buber believes that reality exists only in effective action.
When the mystics attempt to make union with God their goal,
they abandon the responsibility of the I for the Thou. To
strive to become a saint and seek union with God is to give
oneself over to the world of It, a world which uses spiritual
practices and various rituals to bring about a conscious end
result. But reality—both "lived" reality and "inner" reality—

Buber insists, is only found in mutual action. The most powerful and the deepest kind of reality exists where and when, without any reservation, everything enters into the effective action, the whole man as the united I in relation to the all-embracing God, the boundless Thou.[7]

Buber cannot accept mysticism because "the central reality of the everyday hour on earth, with a streak of sun on a maple twig and the glimpse of the eternal Thou, is greater for us than all enigmatic webs on the brink of being." [8] Reality is not to be found in some kind of ecstatic state beyond man's human senses, but rather it is to be found in the whole man and in following the world of the everyday.

> I know nothing of a "world" and a "life in the world" that might separate a man from God. What is thus described is actually life with an alienated world of It, which experiences and uses. He who truly goes out to meet the world goes out also to God. Concentration and outgoing are necessary, both in truth, at once the one and the other, which is the One.
>
> God comprises, but is not, the universe. So, too, God comprises, but is not, my Self. In view of the inadequacy of any language about this fact, I can say Thou in my language as each man can in his, in view of this I and Thou live, and dialogue and spirit and language (spirit's primal act), and the Word in eternity.[9]

The world of the It is a powerful one, Buber believes, while the world of the Thou is extremely delicate. When a living person rises out of the world of things—the world of It—and by his nearness and speech relates to another as a Thou, inevitably the span of time that he remains a Thou is short. "It is not the relation that necessarily grows feeble, but the actuality of its immediacy." [10] Even love cannot continue in the immediate relation. It endures only in the interchange of actual being and potential being. Every Thou by its nature becomes a thing for everyone, or continually re-enters the conditions of things.

It is only in "one, all-embracing relation" that potential being is always actual being. There is only one Thou that cannot by its very nature be anything to us other than a Thou. The person who knows God may very well feel remote from him and feel anguish in his heart, but he can never know the absence of God, for God is always there, even though we may not be.[11]

> The world of It is set in the context of space and time.
>
> The world of Thou is not set in the context of either of these.
>
> Its context is in the Centre, where the extended lines of relations meet—in the eternal Thou.[12]

Whenever pure relation is established, the world of the It is abolished. The world of Thou comes into existence and isolated experiences of pure relation are bound up in "a life of world solidarity." The Thou can transform the world of It. We do not have to be alienated from the world or lose touch with reality. By turning to the Center—to the eternal Thou—we are able to discover the real experience of relation and give new life to the world.[13]

There are three aspects to Buber's philosophy of the I-Thou. First there is the fluctuation that exists between the I-Thou and the I-It relationships. Second, there is the interplay between meeting the eternal Thou and going out from the meeting into the world of men and of the everyday. Third, there is the interplay between the relationship with the eternal Thou which results in a revelation and a turning in which man turns from the restricting and codified forms of religion to a personal,

direct confrontation and meeting with the eternal Thou. Buber
sees good as that which results when the world of the It is
permeated by I-Thou because of a continual return to the
eternal Thou. Evil is seen as the superior of I-It over I-Thou
in the world due to a lack of contact with the eternal Thou.
But Buber believes that the influence of I-It in the world, the
turning away from God, can be used to fulfill God's purposes
by making men aware of the value of I-Thou in the world.

The world of relation is built in three spheres, says Buber.
Our life with nature, our life with men, and our life with
spiritual beings (i.e., art, music—not spiritual beings in a
religious sense). In each sphere we are able to meet and
address the eternal Thou. "Every sphere is compassed in the
eternal Thou, but it is not compassed in them." [14]

The most important sphere, however, is our life with men.
It is in this sphere that we find speech, and in the give-and-take
of talk we are able to express the relation of the I to the Thou.

> The moments of relation are here, and only here, bound to-
> gether by means of the element of the speech in which they are
> immersed. Here what confronts us has blossomed into the full
> reality of the Thou. Here alone, then, as reality that cannot be
> lost, are gazing and being gazed upon, knowing and being
> known, loving and being loved. [15]

It is our life with man that "is the main portal, into whose
opening the two sidegates lead, and in which they are included." The relation with man is like the relation with God
because "in it true address receives true response." But there
is one exception. When God responds, everything in the universe is made manifest as language.

Solitude may also be a gate to God, Buber states. There

are times in "stillest loneliness" when we experience "an un-
suspected perception." But solitude, if it is to be used to meet
God, must never be a time of isolation in which a man speaks
only to himself. It must be a time of purification for the man
who is bound in relation. For only he who is bound in relation with others can confront the reality of God.[16]

Man has many "idols" which are some sort of finite good,
such as a nation, art, power, knowledge, money, or "the
ever-new subjugation of woman." These have become an absolute value in his life and stand between him and God. It
is thought that if he is shown how temporary all these things
are, his idol will be shattered, and the religious act that has
been diverted will automatically return to fill his life. This
presupposes that man's relation to his "idolized" finite things
is the same as is his relation to God and that only the object
is different.

But man's relationship to a "special something" that replaces the supreme value in life, a something that replaces
eternity, rests on a relationship to an It. And a relationship
with an It obscures and obstructs the possibility of relation
with God. It is when man develops a relationship in which he
says Thou that the way is open to God. Whenever a man is
dominated by a possession, there is only one way to God, and
that is by turning. A man must change the nature of his movement. Possession of things can never lead a man toward
God; he must be saved by being awakened and educated to
solidarity of relation.[17]

What does it mean, Buber asks, if a man treats money,
"embodied non-being," as if it were God? What does acquir-
ing material treasure have in common with the joy of being
in God's presence? Can a person say Thou to money? And

how is a man ever able to relate to God if he is not able to say Thou? No man can serve two masters, not even consecutively. A man must learn to serve differently if he would serve God.

The danger in making an idol of a possession, a thing that can be held, is that a man may call it God. But God cannot be held. "Woe to the man so possessed that he thinks he possesses God!" [18] Finite goods mean possessing and using something, while the infinite, eternal Thou cannot be possessed or used.

It has been said that the religious man is one who does not have to be involved with the world or with living beings; that he stands as a single, isolated, separated being before God. But this is not true. Relation with God cannot be separated from relation with man. One relation is never removed from another. All are part of universal relation. Life, therefore, cannot be divided between a real relation with God and an unreal relation between the I and the It of the world. You cannot truly pray to God and profit by the world. Whoever knows the world as something from which he is to profit also knows God in the same way. He is the godless man, not the "atheist," who addresses the Nameless out of the night and yearning of his garret window. In order for a man to have a relation with the eternal Thou he must have a relation with the Thou of the world. [19]

When man meets the eternal Thou he is exposed to a revelation. By that Buber means that the moment of supreme meeting is a phenomenon which somehow affects a man's life.

> The moment of meeting is not an "experience" that stirs in the receptive soul and grows to perfect blessedness; rather, in that moment something happens to the man. At times it is like a

light breath, at times like a wrestling-bout, but always—it happens. The man who emerges from the act of pure relation that so involves his being has now in his being something more that has grown in him, of which he did not know before and whose origin he is not rightly able to indicate.[20]

The man who meets God receives what he did not have before the meeting and he knows that it has been given to him. It is not a specific content, however, but "a Presence, a Presence as power." This Presence and power are composed of three things which are undivided, but they can be considered separately. First, there is a real mutual action that occurs. A man meets God and is bound up in relation. He is not certain how this is brought about, nor does it lighten his life. Instead, it makes it heavier with meaning. Secondly, meaning is assured. Nothing can ever again be meaningless. The question about this meaning of life is gone. Thirdly, this meaning is in relation to this world, confirmed in this life. It has nothing to do with the next life.

Having experienced meaning, however, Buber feels that it cannot be transmitted and made into knowledge available to everyone. Every man discovers the meaning in his own way when he meets God. But the discovery does not lessen its mysteriousness. We come near to God but do not solve the riddle of being. We feel release but no solution.

> The Word of revelation is I am that am. That which reveals is that which reveals. That which is is, and nothing more. The eternal source of strength streams, the eternal contact persists, the eternal voice sounds forth, and nothing more.[21]

Too often when a man meets God, Buber believes, he concerns himself with God. God becomes an object to be sought through devotional exercises. But meeting with God occurs so that a man may confirm that there is meaning in the world. "All revelation is summons and sending." God remains present in a man's life when he is sent forth. When a man goes on a mission after having met God, it is then that God remains near and constant. Those who strive to make God an object in their lives lose Him.[22]

The mighty revelations of God which are the basis of the world's greatest religions are the same in being as the quiet revelations that can be found everywhere and at all times in individual lives. A revelation does not come into the world through a person as though he were a funnel; instead it seizes his whole being and becomes fused to him. A man who receives such a revelation is not a "speaking tube" for the revelation, but rather an organ which sounds according to its own laws.

Throughout the various ages of history man learns of God in differing ways. This occurs not because of man's own power or even God's, but because of a mixture of the two. The form that God takes throughout the course of history is also a mixture of Thou and It. Form in belief, or in a cult, can harden into an object, but if the quality of relation continues to live in it, it continually becomes present again. God is near in his various forms as long as true prayer continues to exist in a belief or a cult. When prayer degenerates, religion degenerates, and it becomes increasingly difficult for man to say Thou to God within the context of religion. He, the man, must finally leave the false security of the religious community and venture alone into the final solitude of the infinite.

Unless a man removes God's forms from God, God is always near them. If, as the religious movement grows in the world, the act of turning is suppressed, the form is removed from God. God no longer knows it and the spiritually understood universe crashes in. This is how the revelation of the eternally present God occurs and reoccurs in history.

Buber believes history to be a "mysterious approach." It leads man into "profounder perversion" but also a deeper and more basic turning. But while man sees the moment he begins to move toward God as turning, God views the moment as redemption.[23]

IV. Hasidism

It is not too much to say that one of the greatest influences—if not the greatest—in Buber's life was Hasidism. Its teachings and legends provided the style and substance for all of his work. It would therefore be impossible to understand fully Buber and his thought without some understanding of the Hasidic movement.

The Hebrew word *hasid* means "pious." And those who belong to the movement are known as Hasidim, those who are loyal to the covenant, or those who are truly pious. The Hasidic movement came into existence in the eighteenth century in Poland, and in spite of bitter persecution by traditional Rabbinism, it seized eastern European Jewry until at one time almost half of all Jews in that part of the world were part of the movement. "In a century which was . . . not very productive religiously," Buber writes, "obscure Polish and Ukrainian Jewry produced the greatest phenomenon we know in the history of the spirit, something which is greater than any solitary genius in art or in the world of thought, a society which lives in faith." [1]

Hasidism developed as a completely Jewish movement, but one which reacted against the worst aspects of the Judaism of its day. However, to understand Hasidism we must briefly delve into the history of the Jews in Poland in the years before its emergence.

In 1648 Polish Jews were subjected to one of the most extreme persecutions that the Jews have ever known. In that year a Cossack by the name of Bogdan Chmielnitki led an army of peasants in an attempt to rise up against their Polish landlords. As this army of peasants attempted to achieve its objectives, its hatred and animosity fell upon another group besides the landed aristocracy, the innocent Jewish townsfolk who often worked as stewards for the landlords. For a decade, until 1658, the Jewish community was devastated and destroyed. It was estimated that over 100,000 Jewish lives were lost during that period of time. The massacres that occurred were equal to the most terrible experienced by the Jews between the seventeenth and twentieth centuries. Along with rape and murder, thousands were left homeless.

The Jews in Poland turned to their ancient hope for a messiah to deliver them from their agony. They thought they had found their deliverer in one Sabbatai Sevi (1625–1676). Sabbatai Sevi was a rather undistinguished individual who had an apparent psychosis, generally having been considered a manic depressive. Partly because of the charisma that he generated during moments of great exaltation, but due more primarily to his association with a mystic named Nathan of Gaza, who acted as his chief propagandist, Sabbatai Sevi brought not only the Jews of Poland but many other European Jewish communities to a fever pitch of messianic expectation during the 1660s.

By 1666, when Sabbatai Sevi proclaimed himself the messiah, countless Jews in Poland and elsewhere had disposed of all their material possessions because they expected that the "messiah" would at any instant cause a miracle to occur and they would all be carried to Israel where Sabbatai Sevi had already established the "messianic era." Confronted by the Turkish authorities and faced with possible martyrdom, he chose conversion to the Moslem faith.

Needless to say, the impact that his conversion had on his followers was shattering. But in parts of eastern Europe and especially in Poland, as unbelievable as it may seem, his movement continued to exist. His loyal followers stated that only by defying the traditional practices of Judaism would the messianic hope be fulfilled. By converting to Islam, Sabbatai Sevi was setting an example for all.

And so Sabbatianism continued, but mostly as an underground movement, because of the opposition to it by established Judaism.[2]

The Kabbalah, a tradition of secret learning found within Jewish mysticism and based on teachings that seem to have existed before the time of Christ, not only had a spiritual and contemplative side, it also had a practical one whose purpose it was to bring about changes in history. The most common of its practical historical goals was to bring about the coming of the Messiah. It was this practical side of the Kabbalah which was the basis for the superstitions and weird practices of Sabbatianism. Because of the heretical aspects of many of the Kabbalah's doctrines, the rabbis feared its influence. However, by the time of the Baal Shem-Tov—the

founder of Hasidism—despite its excesses, the tradition of
the Kabbalah had brought into existence a number of books
which greatly influenced Jewish thought and practice.

Rabbi Israel ben Eliezer of Mezbizk (1700–1760), who
became the Baal Shem-Tov—the Master of the Good Name—
was a teacher, but not in the ordinary sense of the word. Although a number of works were written which attempted to
preserve the actual words spoken by the Baal Shem-Tov, they
are filled with inaccuracies and reflect more the writer's imagi-
native enthusiasm rather than the Baal Shem's remarks.

More than a teaching, Hasidism is a form of community.
The Baal Shem was able to take the teachings of the Kabbalah
and form a popular religious movement that proved suc-
cessful in responding to the challenge presented by the messianism of Sabbatianism. He was able to take the mystical
thought found in the Kabbalah and fill it with an ethical foundation and thereby use the great religious upheaval of his
time to bring into existence "the greatest phenomenon we
know in the history of the spirit."

The Baal Shem attempted to bring to the Jewish people
one basic message that he derived from the Kabbalah and
that message was that every single part of existence has within
it a spark of the divine. All of existence is filled with a potential holiness and it is every man's responsibility to fulfill
and make real that potential.

Hasidism was able to preserve the messianic ardor of the
people, but it diverted their concern away from the future to
a concern for God and man in the present. It taught that it
was the present in which was to be found redemption. It took
the doctrines of the Kabbalah and infused them with a new
and warm feeling for life and existence. It changed the emphasis from speculation to a concern about the individual soul

and its attempts at purification. It stressed the need to cleave to God in the everyday moments of life and the need to do good.

> The simple man, whom the hasidic teaching praises, has not a particle of self-consciousness. He would consider himself ridiculed if told that he was chosen. He too has no need to decide, for he lives his life quite simply, without any subtle inquiries; he accepts the world as it is, and wherever the opportunity comes to him, he does the good which is entrusted to him with an undaunted soul, as if he had known it from all eternity; if, however, he once should go astray, then he seeks with all his might for a way out and casts his lot on God. It is God he cares for, He is his great Lord and Friend; as Lord and Friend he addresses Him continuously, he tells Him everything, as if God knew nothing of it; he is not embarrassed in His presence.[3]

Buber believed that the first and foremost principle of Hasidism was that life should be filled with fervor and exalted joy. He felt that a man should do his daily work eagerly, repeating the Psalms that he has memorized, knowing this as a way of speaking to God and knowing that God would listen and that sometimes if the simple man feels particularly glad in his heart and whistles or dances or even jumps in God's honor because he knows no other way to show his love, then God will rejoice over the man and his actions. The God of Hasidism knows how to rejoice as do his Hasidim.[4]

The strength of the Hasidic movement and the primary reason for its spectacular growth during the first fifty years of its existence was due to the *zaddik*, the spiritual leader in every Hasidic community whose charisma and faith attracted and held together the Hasidim, his disciples. The Hasidic community who belong to a particular *zaddik* form a powerful dynamic unit. The *zaddik* unites with his circle of disciples in prayer and teaching. When he prays, the community is his point of departure. He does not pray for them as their spokesman, but acts as the focus of their faith. The soul of the community unites in strength with his soul. At the third meal on the Sabbath, the *zaddik* reads the Scriptures and interprets them for his disciples. He directs his teaching toward them so that the spirit of what he says reaches into their lives and goes out into ever-expanding circles much like the rings in water after a pebble has been dropped into it.[5]

Unfortunately, that which made Hasidism strong eventually made it weak. The *zaddikim* were great spiritual men, but over a period of time they acquired great power and this led eventually to the establishment of aristocratic dynasties. At first, the *zaddik* was not above his disciples. He was their guide, seeking ways to lead them to that place where they could experience genuine relationship with each other and with God. But the *zaddik* degenerated as a spiritual leader, and religious faith and enthusiasm were replaced by superstition and an unconcern for religious growth. The *zaddik* eventually came to live in oriental luxury and exploited the faith of the simple Jewish followers who acknowledged his leadership.

Buber attempted to capture the genius of the Hasidic movement during its early golden period from approximately 1750 to 1825, collecting and preserving for future generations its many tales and stories.

It must be seen that Buber's reading of Hasidism is very selective, as are his interpretations. When we read about Hasidism in Buber's works, we are not getting a complete picture, but only the best elements of the movement as he sees them; we are looking at Hasidism as Buber beheld it and not in any balanced historical sense.

Through the Hasidic tales Buber attempted to show that God was not so much concerned about whether a man performed the external practices of religion as he was that a man's goal in life was to fulfill God's will in the everyday activities of living. It was the consecration of all that a person did in his everyday existence—the following of the everyday—that was of supreme importance. As Buber stated in his preface to *Ten Rungs: Hasidic Sayings:* "For there is no rung of being on which we cannot find the holiness of God everywhere and at all times."

One of the Hasidic tales most often quoted because of its lesson of following the everyday and emphasizing the way real concerns and love take precedence over the externals of religion is seen in a story entitled "The Delay" from Buber's second volume of the *Tales of the Hasidim.*

> On the eve of the Day of the Atonement when the time had come to say Kol Nidre (the most solemn time of prayer in the Jewish year) all the hasidim were gathered together in the House of Prayer waiting for the rabbi. But time passed and he did not come. Then one of the women of the congregation said to herself: "I guess it will be quite a while before they begin, and I was in such a hurry and my child is alone in the house. I'll just run home and look after it to make sure it hasn't awakened. I can be back in a few minutes."
>
> She ran home and listened at the door. Everything was quiet. Softly she turned the knob and put her head into the room—and there stood the rabbi holding her child in his arms. He had heard the child crying on his way to the House of Prayer, and had played with it and sung to it until it fell asleep.[6]

In a preface to one of his smaller volumes, Buber very succinctly described Hasidism. In most systems of belief, he stated, the believer feels that if he is able to renounce the world of his senses and overcome his own natural being he will be able to achieve a perfect relationship with God. But the Hasid thinks differently. He believes that "cleaving" to God should be man's highest aim in life, but that he does not have to abandon the external and internal reality of earthly being in order to reach that relationship. He must, instead, affirm being in its "true, God-oriented essence" and thereby change it so that it can be offered up to God.

Buber has always made it clear that Hasidism is not pantheism. It believes in the absolute transcendence of God, but this must also be seen as being combined with a "conditioned immanence." The world radiates God, but there is an independence to existence and the world is apt to form a crust around itself. And so, Buber believes—with the Hasid—that a divine spark lives in every thing and in every being, but this spark is covered by an outer shell that isolates it. Only man can break that shell and set that spark free and in that way help to "rejoin" it with the origin of all things, God. Man can do this by relating to the thing or being in a holy way; that is, if his intention is to relate to all things while bearing in mind that he directs his efforts toward God's transcendence, then the divine immanence can emerge from out of the shells.

But more important is the fact that in every man is a divine force. And man, more than all other living beings, can pervert and misuse that divine force found in himself. If man allows that divine force to run in any direction rather than directing it in the direction of its origin, it becomes evil instead of becoming hallowed. But there is a way to be redeemed. If man "turns" to God with his whole being, he will be able to lift the divine immanence out of the debased state into which he has placed it. "The task of man, of every man, according to Hasidic teaching," Buber concludes, "is to affirm for God's sake the world and himself and by this very means to transform both." [7]

Buber believes that the idea of turning to God and being lifted to new heights stands at the center of the Jewish conception of man. Turning is able to renew a man from within and change his position in God's world. It is able to raise him above sin. By turning, Buber means something much more than just repentance, for the act encompasses the reversal of a man's whole being. He is able, through turning, to find a way to God and to leave behind a life centered on self, but without acts of penance. Anyone concerned with repentance is not able to give all his energies to the work of reversal. Buber refers in his writing to the Rabbi of Gar, who gave a sermon on the Day of Atonement and warned against self-torture. The thrust of the sermon was that a person is what he thinks. If a man sins and his thoughts constantly dwell on his sins, then the man will always dwell in baseness and constantly be overcome by gloom. No matter how you "rake the muck," it will always be muck. It does not matter whether you have sinned or not sinned, "what does heaven get out of it?" The only way to counteract wrong is by doing right. [8]

The way to best understand the spirit of Hasidism as Buber experienced it is to delve into the stories and sayings of the movement as he preserved them. What follows are examples which capture the feel, if not the essence, of his tales:

The Horses

In the course of their long wanderings, the two brothers Rabbi Zusya and Rabbi Elimelekh often came to the city of Ludmir. There they always slept in the house of a poor, devout man. Years later, when their reputation had spread all over

the country, they came to Ludmir again, not on foot as before, but in a carriage. The wealthiest man in that little town,
who had never wanted to have anything to do with them, came
to greet them, the moment he heard they had arrived, and
begged them to lodge in his house. But they said: "Nothing
has changed in us to make you respect us more than before.
What is new is just the horses and the carriage. Take them for
your guests, but let us stop with our old host, as usual." [9]

Who May Be Called Man?

Concerning the words in the Scriptures: "When any man of
you bringeth an offering to the Lord . . ." the rabbi of Rizbyn
said: "Only he who brings himself to the Lord as an offering
may be called man." [10]

Depending on God

Rabbi Moshe Leib said: "How easy it is for a poor man to
depend on God. What else has he to depend on? And how
hard it is for a rich man to depend on God! All his possessions
call out to him: 'Depend on us!' " [11]

His Bad Foot

In his youth Rabbi Hayyim Zans was a disciple of the Zaddik
of Roptchitz. His fervor in praying was so great that he
stamped on the floor with both feet. But one foot was lame.
Once when the Zaddik's wife had watched Hayyim pray, she
went to her husband and said: "What a heartless person you
are! Why do you let him pound the floor with his bad foot?
Tell him to use only his good foot."

"I could do that right enough," answered the Zaddick, "if, in
praying, he knew every time whether he was using his good
or his bad foot." [12]

The Great Crime

Rabbi Bunam said to his hasidim: "The sins which man

commits—those are not his great crime. Temptation is powerful and his strength is slight! The great crime of man is that he can turn (to God) at every moment, and does not do so." [13]

Zusya and the Birds

Once Rabbi Zusya traveled cross-country collecting money to ransom prisoners. He came to an inn at a time when the innkeeper was not at home. He went through the rooms, according to custom, and in one saw a large cage with all kinds of birds. And Zusya saw that the caged creatures wanted to fly through the spaces of the world and be free birds again. He burned with pity for them and said to himself: "Here you are, Zusya, walking your feet off to ransom prisoners. But what greater ransoming of prisoners can there be than to free these birds from their prison?" Then he opened the cage, and the birds flew out into freedom.

When the innkeeper returned and saw the empty cage, he was very angry, and asked the people in the house who had done this to him. They answered: "A man is loitering about here and he looks like a fool. No one but he can have done this thing." The innkeeper shouted at Zusya: "You fool! How could you have the impudence to rob me of my birds and make worthless the good money I paid for them?" Zusya replied: "You have often read and repeated these words in the psalms: 'His tender mercies are over all His works.'" Then the innkeeper beat him until his hand grew tired and finally threw him out of the house. And Zusya went his way serenely. [14]

The Hasidic stories that Buber preserved for the Western world always deal with ordinary events which become extraordinary because they give the reader, or listener, a deeper understanding of the meaning of life and of man's relationship to God. They describe occurrences which are changed in such a way as to give answers to questions which are basic to human life. They are similar to the stories in Scripture which should be read over and over again in order to get their full meaning. The conclusion of each tale is reached in a spirit of innocence, and it is only by reading the great range of stories that one is able to get the full impact of their conclusions. In an indirect way they speak a greater truth than the obvious ones found in each of the tales, a truth that can be sensed and known but never clearly expressed.

Hasidism was interpreted by Buber as being able to heal the breach that exists between the profane and the holy, between the world and God. He accepted the realities of life and rejected asceticism and melancholy. Joy in life was seen by Buber to be a reflection of the divine. His emphasis was that life was good with all of its evil, sin, and sorrow. The message of Hasidism, as he saw it, was a liberating one. Through his interpretation of the movement he brought to Western man the message that there is a divine grace that gives man an opportunity to take part in God's coming to the world.

V. Martin Buber and the Bible

One of Buber's main scholarly interests—as would be expected—was interpreting the Bible. In his later years this was his major concern. In 1961, he completed the translation of the Hebrew Bible into German, the work he had begun with Franz Rosenzweig thirty-six years earlier in 1925.

Buber believed that his philosophy of dialogue had its foundation in the Bible and even tended to interpret the Bible on the basis of that philosophy. He saw that the Bible (the Hebrew Bible—the Old Testament) was a book composed of many books united by one basic theme: the sequence of events that occurred on earth in the course of history as a group of people encountered God in their lives. He believed that the stories of the Bible, its songs and prophecies, are either openly or by implication reports of these encounters.

Since the Bible was written, every generation has been forced to struggle with it. Even though the generations are not always ready to respond to it positively, "the preoccupation with this book is part of their life and they face it in

the realm of reality." [1] Even when the Bible is denied, the
very act of denying it bears witness to it.[2]

Buber sees the man of today in relation to the Bible as
basically an intellectually oriented person. Even his obligations of the spirit are only intellectual. It is a reflection of our
time that there are no obligations imposed on man by the
things of the spirit. Man speaks about the rights of the spirit,
and develops laws for it, but these are found in books and
not in the lives of men. Things of the spirit "float in mid-air
above our heads, rather than walk the earth in our midst.
Everything except everyday life belongs to the realm of the
spirit." [3]

There is a false relationship between everyday life and the
spirit. Buber believes there should instead be a union of both.
While these two "interdependent entities" should not be separated, they actually are. The spirit is seen either as "spurious
idealism" toward which men gaze without obligation to have
it affect their lives, or as "spurious realism" which changes
the unconditional nature of the spirit into a number of condi-
tional characters, some of which are psychological, socio-
logical, and others. There are some who realize the danger
that this separation of the spirit and everyday life has on the
spirit. It can be corroded until it is "debased into a willing
and complacent servant of whatever powers happen to rule the
world." How can this be prevented? Those who have been concerned see religion as the only force capable of bringing together a new union between the world and the spirit. But
religion as it exists today could never accomplish the task,
Buber tells us. In our present circumstances, religion has become a part of the detached spirit. It belongs to that which is
seen as being above life and is not an entity that includes all
of life.[4]

In order for religion again to influence men, it must return to reality. Religion has only been real in the past when it sanctified everyday life, was free of fear, and was willing to accept the concrete. It is in the Old Testament that the reality of which Buber speaks is to be found. The Old Testament has two traits that set it apart from other great religions, he feels. One trait is that the events of the Old Testament are to be found in the life of a people living in the world. The holy becomes a part of history, and is reflected in the lives of a community of people whose example may serve as a model for others in different times and in different places. The second trait is reflected in the laws found in the Old Testament: they affect the natural course of a man's life. Man is told what he is to eat and how he is to live in the marital state, among so many other things, but he is always accepted for what he is, with all his passions and urges. Holiness is always seen as a part of man's existence.[5]

The Old Testament functions as a witness to the spirit's desire to be perfect and to the command that man must serve the spirit in its search for union with life. If the Old Testament is seen only as religious writing it loses its significance. It must be recognized as a reflection of a reality that encompasses all of life. Contemporary man, however, if he is at all interested in Scripture, is often interested in an abstract sense. His is an aesthetic interest, or one connected with the history of civilization, or the history of religion. Man today does not stand before the biblical Word as he has in generations past, either to respond to it or to be offended by it. He does not judge his life by the Word, but rather hides it in a compartment so that it is not affected by the biblical Word, and he is relieved. "Thus he paralyzes the power that, of all powers, is best able to save him." [6]

The man of today, Buber feels, does not have access to a "sure and solid faith." When he reads the Bible, he is not always able to believe it. The faith that is necessary to grasp the Bible's true message is often missing and is not accessible to modern man. So there is only one thing that he can do and that is to hold himself open to faith. "If he is really serious, he too can open up to this book and let its rays strike him where they will." [7]

In order to achieve a true perception of the meaning of the Bible, it must be read as if it were completely unfamiliar. One must approach the Bible as if it were something entirely new to him. He must not be influenced by past concepts; he must give himself to it entirely without holding back any aspect of his very being, and then he must allow whatever will happen between himself and the Bible to happen.

> He does not know which of its sayings and images will overwhelm him and mold him, from where the spirit will ferment and enter into him, to incorporate itself anew in his body. But he holds himself open. He does not believe anything a priori; he does not disbelieve anything a priori. He reads aloud the words written in the book in front of him; he hears the word he utters and it reaches him. Nothing is prejudged. The current of time flows on, and the contemporary character of this man becomes itself a receiving vessel. [8]

There is a complete chasm existing today between man and the Scriptures. The Bible has always confronted every generation with the claim that within its contents is to be found the true history of the world; a history that indicates the world's origin and goal. Scripture demands that every person must integrate his own life into that history and find his origin in the origin of the world and his goal in the goal of the world. The Jewish Bible (and Buber has only been referring

to the Old Testament), however, does not have an established midpoint between origin and goal.[9]

> It interposes a movable, circling midpoint which cannot be
> pinned to any set time, for it is the moment when I, the reader,
> the hearer, the man, catch through the words of the Bible the
> voice which from earliest beginnings has been speaking in the
> direction of the goal. The midpoint is this mortal and yet im-
> mortal moment of mine. Creation is the origin, redemption the
> goal. But revelation is not a fixed, dated point poised between
> the two. The revelation at Sinai is not this midpoint itself, but
> the perceiving of it, and such perception is possible at any
> time. That is why a psalm or a prophecy is no less Torah,
> i.e., instruction, than the story of the exodus from Egypt. The
> history of this people—accepting and refusing at once—points
> to the history of all mankind, but the secret dialogue expressed
> in the psalms and prophecies points to my own secret.[10]

Man today has two approaches to history. He may view it
as a hodgepodge of shifting events, a medley of actions which
give an unreliable and unsubstantial semblance of meaning.
Or he may see history from a dogmatic point of view, deriv-
ing laws from past events and thereby calculating future
events. History is not a living, vital, constantly moving sequence of events into which a man must interject his time and
his decisions, but rather is seen as "stark, ever-present, in-
escapable space."

Both of these views of history must be recognized as mis-
interpretations, Buber tells us. According to the Bible, history
and "historic destiny" are the secret correlations inhering in
the current moment. There is no meaningless drifting in life
when we are aware of origin and goal. We become a part of a
meaning which we are to live, a meaning which we do not
formulate. And we live in the "awful and splendid moment
of decision."

But man today does not know of a beginning nor of an
end. Man is unable to see an origin or a goal because he
does not wish to recognize a midpoint. Man resists Scripture
because he cannot bear revelation, and creation and redemption are only true when revelation is an experience of the
present. To accept revelation is to be able to accept the present
moment with its possibilities for decision; to be able and willing to respond to the moment and be responsible for it. And
man today does not want to accept responsibility, so he resists the Bible.[11]

Buber believes that we begin to understand the Bible when
we see a distinction between creation, revelation and redemption. These three must be seen as stages in the course of
God's relationship with the world and as the main directions
of his movement toward the world. But creation, revelation,
and redemption must not be seen as separate entities. Bibli-
cally, creation is in the beginning, revelation is in the middle,
and redemption is in the end. But the truth is that they coincide.
Every day the work of the beginning is renewed by God but
every day also anticipates the end. It is only when revelation
is seen as a present experience that creation and redemption
are true. If we were not able to experience creation and redemption in our own lives, we would never be able to understand what they are.[12]

We must start at this point, Buber says, if we are to bridge
the chasm between man and the Bible. It is possible for man
to hold himself open to faith, but is not the strangeness of
biblical concepts and ideas a stumbling block? Has not man
in his theory of evolution lost the reality of creation; and in
the theory of the unconscious, revelation; and by establishing
social or national goals, redemption?

There is a substantial quality to the strangeness of biblical

concepts and we must understand it before we attempt to
show that there is still an approach to faith through the Bible.

How do we interpret such biblical events as God coming
down in fire; that in the midst of thunder and the sound of
the horn, he descended to a mountain which was smoking
like a furnace and spoke to his people? What is the true
meaning of these occurrences?

Buber believes they can mean one of three things. First,
the words could be interpreted as figurative language which is
used to express a "spiritual" process, that is, the events in
the Scripture did not actually happen but are really metaphor
and allegory. But the events then would not be biblical and
should be surrendered to modern man's historical or aesthetic
interpretations.

There could be a second meaning: that the events of the
Bible are supernatural and sever the intelligible occurrence
of natural happenings and interject something unintelligible.
If that were the case, then in order to accept the events of
the Bible, a man would have to sacrifice his intellect when
reading it. A man would then only be accepting religion abstracted from life instead of all of life as it is found in its
totality in the Bible.

But there is a third possibility. The events of Scripture
could be the "verbal trace of a natural event." Buber means
by this that certain events took place that affected the senses
of all involved in such a way that they were only able to perceive them by interpreting them in a certain way. Those who
experienced the events saw them as occurring because God
had caused them to happen. God brought a revelation to those
involved and it was accepted as such by one generation after
another. This may seem at first to be self-delusion, but it is
not. Natural events are the means whereby revelations are

seen, and when those who view these events recognize and perceive with their reason that they are experiencing a revelation, then it is so. It is only when a man is listening to the voice that speaks out of an event and it is able to speak to his life and his sense of duty that a man can find the approach to biblical reality.[13]

We sometimes have personal experiences that are very similar to biblical revelations. These experiences make it possible for us to understand the biblical revelations, Buber believes. Quite unexpectedly we may become aware of an apperception within ourselves, an apperception which did not exist a moment before and whose origin is unknown to us. There are psychological ways of interpreting the apperception, but Buber prefers to interpret it as "otherness, the touch of the other." We are given a gift and we must accept it as such, otherwise we are involved in theft. Only when we are aware that we have been given a gift and accept it as such are we then able to "set foot on the path that will reveal our life and the life of the world as a sign communication. This path is the approach." It is on the same path where our minor experience is encountered that we will meet with our major experience.

Only as we are able to perceive revelation, says Buber, are we able to perceive creation and redemption. When we question our own origin and goal in life, we are also questioning the origin and goal of something other than ourselves, something other than the world. But in this questioning we begin to recognize the origin and goal of the world.[14]

How are we to interpret the biblical pronouncement that God created the world in six days? That does not mean that God created the world in six ages, Buber contends. Those who attempt to use this interpretation are trying to force the Bible into harmony with current scientific views. This is inadequate, as is the attempt to interpret the acts of creation in a mystical way so as to convert them into emanations. Mysticism resists the idea that God became man for our sakes, but if the Bible is divested of the acting character of God, it loses its significance.

What meaning should we find in the story of creation? Buber asks. While there are no verbal traces that can be read concerning the event since, naturally, no one witnessed it, does that mean that it is not possible to believe in the biblical story of creation unless you believe with a great faith? No, replies Buber. We must recognize, he says, that what is unutterable can only be uttered in the language of men. The story of creation found in the biblical records is a stammering attempt to explain the creation of the world, but it is a legitimate one. Man can only stammer when he attempts to put into order all he knows about the universe and its divine beginning. Stammering is the only way he can do justice to his responsibility of trying to explain the mystery of how, from eternity, time was able to come into existence, and how, from no world, a world was able to come into being. Any attempt to construct a logical scientific explanation for the origin of all things is bound to fail when it is seen in comparison to this.[15]

And so man today is able to approach the reality of revelation, but how does he begin to approach the reality of creation? Looking at his own life does not lead him to creation as readily as it does to revelation, but the reality of creation can be found. It is discovered in man's uniqueness and individuality. Suppose it were possible for a person to take his character apart so that he would have all of his qualities in a separate state. Then suppose he traced each quality back to the most primitive living creatures and then did a genetic analysis of each quality from its earliest beginning until his existence. He would discover that his face, his body, his voice, his gestures and his inner spirit would be the residue of all that had gone on before. He would ultimately realize that he is something that was created. "Because every man is unique, another first man enters the world whenever a child is born. By being alive, everyone groping like a child back to the origin of his own self, we may experience the fact that there is an origin, that there is a creation." [16]

But the most difficult problem to resolve is the last: how can we believe the biblical concept of redemption, the concept that the world will someday be saved and there will be "a new heaven and a new earth" (Isa. 66:22)? Two misconceptions must be avoided, Buber states. Redemption should not be interpreted as referring to another world to come. It means rather that this world will become the Kingdom; that this world will be made perfect. The second misconception is to think of redemption as referring to a more righteous order and mankind becoming more peaceful. For Buber it does not. It means rather that there will be righteousness and peace in the world.

And again we hear legitimate stammering. The prophet speaks only in the words of men. He can only declare what it is from which he will be redeemed and not for what he has been redeemed. But what about the man of today? Does not this all sound strange to him? He has a fathomless yearning. He hopes for change and a new tomorrow, but the coming of truth means nothing to him. Even though he struggles to overcome obstacles, he does not realize that a power is attempting to redeem him and the world from contradiction. He also does not realize that this power demands that the whole of his being be turned. Where does the bridge exist between man and the message of the Bible?

This is the most difficult thing to understand. Although man may receive knowledge of revelation from the lived moment, and reflecting upon his own birth may lead to an understanding of creation, no one will understand the essence of redemption until his final hour.[17]

> And yet here, too, there is an approach. It is dark and silent and cannot be indicated by any means, save by my asking you to recall your own dark and silent hours. I mean those hours in the lowest depths when our soul hovers over the frail trap door which, at the very next instant, may send us down into destruction, madness, and suicide at our own verdict. Indeed, we are astonished that it has not opened up until now. But suddenly we feel a touch as of a hand. It reaches down to us, it wishes to be grasped—and yet what incredible courage is needed to take the hand, to let it draw us up out of the darkness! This is redemption. We must realize the true nature of the experience proffered us: It is that our "redeemer liveth" (Job 19:25), that He wishes to redeem us—but only by our own acceptance of His redemption with the turning of our whole being." [18]

It is at this point, Buber says, that we are able to begin to approach biblical reality.[19]

VI. Judaism and Zionism

The influence of Buber has grown over the years. During his lifetime he was recognized as the representative figure of world Jewry. His cultural, religious, and intellectual contributions affected the lives and thought of all segments of the Jewish community from the young who give their allegiance to Zionism to the liberals and even the orthodox, to whose laws and regulations he did not subscribe. During his lifetime he did more to bring about a rebirth of Judaism than any other Jew. Not just because of his religious philosophy or the fact that he translated the Bible, or even because he preserved many of the Hasidic legends, but also because of his great religious personality which gave leadership during a time when his people were suffering and facing their greatest ordeal—before and during the Second World War. His writings and thought will doubtless influence many future generations of religious, thinking Jews.[1]

Having said that, we must recognize—as has been pointed out in other parts of this introduction to his life and thought—

that Buber cannot be categorized as being representative of organized Judaism. He attempted to take the essence of the Jewish faith and subject it to a searching analysis. Only when he reached conclusions which were acceptable to his own experience and thought would he then subscribe to the belief.

Buber's thinking in regard to Judaism and Zionism is a case in point. There have been many others who have made his emphasis that the individual person must turn away from himself and his selfish concerns and turn to God. But Buber's approach stresses that the individual does not turn in isolation. He is, instead, a part of a larger, genuine community.

It is when we begin to examine his views on Zionism that we are able to understand the great importance he gave to this concept of community among Jewish people. In his earliest writings, at the turn of the century, he saw Judaism as a means whereby the individual Jew could express his creativity. The individual was bound by a blood tie to the spirit of his people—in the past, the present, and the future.

By the time the Nazis had risen to power in Germany, Buber had abandoned the idea. Influenced by Hasidic teachings and other Jewish thought, he came to see Israel as reflective of the faithfulness of the Jewish people to the Covenant that God had made with the chosen people in the time of Abraham and Moses. Zionism, which was the attempt to bring into existence a Jewish State, became for Buber a way of bringing into being a community based on peace and justice. No longer was he concerned with the effect of Judaism on the individual, but rather he emphasized that God was waiting for mankind to complete the creation he had begun. Man's responsibility was to hallow this world.[2]

During an address given at the National Conference of Palestinian Teachers Association held at Tel Aviv in 1939,

Buber spoke of the *halutz*, the Palestinian pioneer, as "the most striking example of the new Jewish type." The *halutz* works to bring about a social synthesis, a uniting of people living together in a community based on direct and just relations between all members of that community.

The *halutz* receives his inspiration and determination to bring into existence this ideal community from an ancient Jewish longing. Israel was not just an historical or a biological development; it resulted from a decision made long ago favoring a God of justice. The early Jews believed that God had led them into the land of Canaan so that they might be prepared to carry on the messianic work he had planned for them in the world.

Hasidism, Buber believed, was one of the great efforts made by the Jewish people to establish a just community founded on religious beliefs and principles. Although it failed, it did attempt to turn the original choice of the Jews into a reality. Its failure came about because the movement had little connection with Palestine and it was not motivated by a desire for national liberation for the Jews. It was the modern Jewish national movement which finally took up the ancient social message and worked to educate the new type of man, the man who would give life to his ideas, the man who would work to bring into existence a new nation and along with it fulfill the longing for a communal life based on justice.[3]

On November 26, 1938, Mahatma Gandhi published a statement in his newspaper, the *Harijan*, advising the Jews in Germany to use Satyagraha (soul-force) in response to atrocities committed by the Nazis. He was also critical of Zionism and of the fact that the Jews were settling in Palestine and unjustly treating the Arabs who were in possession of land.

Buber took a long time to compose his reply to Gandhi

and after indicating why he believed Satyagraha could not be practiced by the Jews against the Nazis—primarily because the problems faced by Indians in South Africa, where Gandhi had used Satyagraha, were in no way the same as the problems faced by the Jews in Germany—Buber went on to discuss the need of the Jews to return to Palestine.

He emphasized that the destiny of the Jewish people is different from that of all other nations in the world.

> Decisive for us is not the promise of the Land—but the command, the fulfillment of which is bound up with the land, with the existence of a free Jewish community in this country. For the Bible tells us and our inmost knowledge testifies to it, that once, more than three thousand years ago, our entry into this land was in the consciousness of a mission from above to set up a just way of life through the generations of our people, such a way of life as can be realized not by individuals in the sphere of their private existence but only by a nation in the establishment of its society.[4]

Buber goes on to say that the Jewish people went into exile not having fulfilled the command placed upon them and now the command was urgent. But in order to comply with the command, they needed their own land and the freedom to order their own life. "It cannot be that the soil and the freedom for fulfillment are denied us. We are not covetous, Mahatma; our one desire is that at last we may be able to obey." [5]

It is always clear to Buber that man cannot live two separate lives, a secular one and a religious one. Man's dedication must be to God and his commitment must be reflected in his everyday life. It is when man establishes the truly human community that he is showing his commitment to the greatest degree. Buber believed that in true Judaism there is a unified

life on earth. Judaism's goal in the world "is not the creation
of a philosophical theorem or a work of art but the establishment of true community. Herein is grounded the grandeur,
but also the paradox, of Jewish existence." [6]

In response to Gandhi's criticism that the settlement of the
Jews in Palestine was unjust to the Arabs who possessed the
land, Buber attempted to examine Gandhi's thinking. Did
Gandhi mean that because a people were settled in an area
that this automatically gave them absolute claim to the land?
Did he mean that anyone settling on the land without the
permission of those already on it were robbers? But how,
Buber asked, did the Arabs first gain the land? By conquest,
he pointed out. Following the kind of reasoning being pursued
by Gandhi resulted in an awkward conclusion: that settlement
by conquest justified a right to ownership of Palestine, whereas
migratory, peaceful settlement such as was undertaken by the
Jews—although at times not always fair to the Arabs—did
not justify a right to possess the land. The conclusion made
little sense to Buber.[7]

The idea that God is the sole owner of all land is the foundation on which is built the Jewish social concept. It corre-
sponds to the political thought of the Jews that God is the sole
sovereign of the community.[8] "The conquered land is, in my
opinion," says Buber, "only lent even to the conqueror who
has settled on it—and God waits to see what he will make of
it." [9]

Buber concludes his letter to Gandhi by stating that the
land recognizes the Jews, because it has been fruitful to
them. The Jews did not come to Palestine as did other
colonists, making the native inhabitants do the work for
them; they themselves toiled and labored in the fields to make
them fruitful. But a fertile land was not only for the benefit

of the Jews, but also for the benefit of the Arabs. Jewish farmers taught Arab farmers how better to cultivate the land, and further, the Jews did not want to stop with what they had taught the Arabs, but rather wanted to teach them more. They wanted, with the Arabs, to "serve" the land together, for the more fertile the soil became the more space there would be for both peoples. "We have no desire to dispossess them: we want to live with them. We do not want to dominate them, we want to serve with them. . . ." [10]

On September 5, 1921, during the Twelfth Zionist Congress at Karlsbad, Buber gave an address which called for unity with the Arabs if the nation of Israel were ever established. This was always a concern of his in later years, but remarkably, he was first advocating a solution to the Palestine question forty-four years before his death and twenty-seven years before the establishment of the nation of Israel.

In his address, he stated that the desire of the Jews to bring into existence the nation of Israel in their ancient homeland was not aimed against any other people. As they enter world history again and determine their own fate, they reject and abhor the methods of national domination with which for two thousand years they were persecuted as a minority in all the countries of the world. Having suffered for so long, they had no desire to return to the land which was part of their historic and spiritual life to suppress or dominate another people. There was room enough for both peoples, especially if intensive and systematic methods of cultivation were adopted.

Buber foresaw in his address that the return of the Jews to the "Land of Israel" would come through constant growth and increasing immigration, but it would not occur at the expense of another people's rights. He proposed that a just alliance be established with the Arabs so that Israel would

flourish both economically and culturally for the benefit of
both peoples. He hoped that such progress would allow each to
develop independently and unhampered. Buber wanted some
kind of arrangement to be worked out by the Arabs and the
Jews which would be acceptable to both groups and which
would allow them to live as neighbors, in peace with each
other. It was his wish, he said in this early speech, that a
"deep and constant solidarity of genuine interests" would
come into existence and would eventually overcome the op-
posing interests of the Jews and the Arabs. He hoped from all
this that feelings of "mutual respect and goodwill" would
occur in the life of both communities and in the lives of each
of its individual members: "Only then will both peoples meet
in a new and glorious historical encounter." [11]

For the remainder of his life Buber continued to work for
a policy of peace and justice for the Arabs. He accepted the
sovereign existence of Israel and attempted to criticize it from
inside with love and concern. He felt that the breach that
existed between the Jews and the Arabs after independence
had been attained must be healed. He insisted that that was
the only way the people of Israel could act. It would be an
expression of their true nature. He wanted Israel to be more
Jewish, not less.[12]

Even during the year he died, he continued attempting to
get Israel to begin a massive initiative to try to resolve the
problem of the Palestinian Arab refugees. He worked to
defend the civil rights of the Arab citizens of Israel and
demanded that they and the Jewish citizens be given equal
treatment.[13]

Buber saw the Middle East as a land that could be fruitful
for both the Jews and the Arabs. He wanted men to live in

peace with each other. He felt great pain at the discord and the violence, but he never stopped trying to make things better. He felt he could do no less in light of his profound beliefs.

VII. Buber and the Christian Faith

It is an interesting fact that Martin Buber's impact and influence on Christians and Christian thinkers has grown over the years. Men such as John Baille, Karl Barth, Emil Brunner, Friedrich Gogarten, Reinhold Niebuhr, H. Richard Niebuhr, J. H. Oldham, and Paul Tillich, to name just a few, have been among the prominent Christian thinkers to be significantly influenced by him.

J. H. Oldham, one of the leaders of the ecumenical movement, stated:

> I am convinced that it is by opening its mind, and conforming its practice, to the truth which Buber has perceived and so powerfully set forth that the Church can recover a fresh understanding of its own faith, and regain a real connection with the actual life of our time.[1]

Paul Tillich, in writing of Buber's significance for Christian theology, wrote:

> Buber's existential "I-Thou" philosophy . . . should be a
> powerful help in reversing the victory of the "It" over the
> "Thou" and the "I" in present civilization. . . . The "I-Thou"
> philosophy . . . challenging both orthodox and liberal theol-
> ogy, points a way beyond their alternatives.[2]

The late James A. Pike, at one time Bishop of the Episcopal
Diocese of California, knew Buber over the years and, re-
counting their relationship, wrote:

> It is doubtful that many Jews who lived past the time of the
> first century A.D. have been commemorated in the stained glass
> windows of Christian Churches. I know of only two. One is
> Samuel Joseph Isaac Schereschewsky. . . . But he had become
> a Christian—and a bishop. . . . The other was . . . Dr. Martin
> Buber. While I was Bishop of the Episcopal Diocese of Cali-
> fornia we completed the Cathedral (Grace Cathedral in San
> Francisco), and in planning windows for the additional bays
> of the Nave we decided to include Dr. Buber. . . .
> Such a recognition would be appropriate in any case (Dr.
> Buber had been a strong influence on contemporary Christian
> theology, not the least among Anglicans), but it was partic-
> ularly meaningful to me because of our personal friendship and
> the influence he has been on me.[3]

It is difficult to read Buber and not realize that, although
he is a Jewish scholar of great stature, his writing and
thought go beyond his own Judaic interests. His concern primarily is to look at modern man and, regardless of his particular religious affiliation, to attempt to examine and explain
modern man's situation in the world today. It is because of
this that Buber has taken great pains in trying to understand
Christianity. His basic humanity and his sincere desire to
comprehend the thinking and actions of contemporary man
have helped him maintain many warm friendships with
Christian theologians during his lifetime.

Buber's widespread influence on Christian thinkers has

been due primarily to *I and Thou.* Unfortunately, this does not
mean that there has been a widespread understanding of the
philosophy to be found in that little book. In order to grasp
its many meanings, it must be read and reread. Only in that
way will it begin to affect one's thoughts as Buber had
intended. The philosophy in *I and Thou* has been used in
many different ways and, at times, has been greatly distorted.

Some theologians have become so concerned with the philosophy of dialogue that they have completely missed the
emphasis Buber made on a living dialogue. Many Christian
thinkers and theologians have utilized the I-Thou philosophy
to establish a radical dualism between I-Thou and I-It relations which is inconsistent with Buber's thought. Some have
equated I-It with the sinful nature of man, and I-Thou with
the grace and divine love only to be found in Christ.

Although Martin Buber has had a tremendous impact on
Christian thinkers and theologians, it would be a serious error
to think of him in any way as a Christian. His thought is
firmly rooted in Judaism and he draws his strength first, last,
and always from that source. Even though his thinking was
unacceptable to most orthodox Jews, even to the Hasidim
whose heritage he preserved and brought to light in Western
civilization, his message, while intended for all men, addressed itself primarily to the Jewish community. It was from
them that he hoped for a response. The fact that many Christians listened and responded does not in any way negate his
complete dependence upon, and reflection of, his Jewish
heritage.

This is best seen when an examination is made of his
thinking in regard to Christianity. In his most profound book
dealing with the subject, *Two Types of Faith,* we are able to

see the fruits of his lifetime study of the New Testament. In this extensive work, Buber deals not only with the theological differences between Judaism and Christianity but also draws a distinction between the history of Israel and the emergence of the Christian Church.

Emil Brunner sees a threefold purpose as well as a threefold object in the writing of this relatively small book.

1. Using the Old Testament as the basis of his analysis, Buber attempts to show what is the basic religious message of Judaism.

2. He then tries to prove that the message Jesus preached came out of and belonged to the same religious tradition as Judaism.

3. He then attempts to show that the thinking and faith of Paul, in particular, and the other early disciples, in general, are completely separated from the thought and faith of Jesus and Judaism.[4]

Perhaps the best way to grasp his interpretation of Christianity is to examine his understanding of Jesus. From this all else evolves. As a Jew, he cannot accept the incarnation of Christ, but he has always recognized and indicated the tremendous religious significance of Jesus. In 1950, Buber wrote of Jesus in these words:

> From my youth onwards I have found in Jesus my great brother. That Christianity has regarded and does regard him as God and Savior has always appeared to me a fact of the highest importance which for his sake and my own, I must endeavor to understand. . . . My own fraternally open relationship to him has grown ever stronger and clearer, and today I see him more strongly and clearly than ever before. I am more than ever certain that a great place belongs to him in Israel's history of faith and that this place cannot be described by any of the usual categories.[5]

In Christianity, it is believed that Jesus is the midpoint of human history and during his life God revealed himself to man in his greatest revelation. The Christian believes that when he looks at Christ he looks at God. But Buber denies that revelation has a fixed midpoint as far as Judaism is concerned. He believes that the Jewish Bible does not establish a midpoint between the beginning and the conclusion of human existence as Christianity does. Instead, he feels that there is a movable, circling midpoint which cannot be attached to any specific time or to any specific event. It is instead that moment when the Bible reveals to a man the voice which has been speaking from the beginning in the direction of the final goal. Buber views this idea of a fixed midpoint as a basic distinction between the Christian and the Jewish understanding of biblical faith.[6]

Buber makes a second distinction between the two faiths: Christianity affirms an entirely "realized" eschatology while Judaism affirms an entirely "futuristic" one. Christianity looks for the return of Christ. The final chapter of the Book of Revelation in the New Testament ends on this expectation: "Come, Lord Jesus!" [7] Judaism believes, however, that a great act of redemption has already occurred when the people of Israel were delivered from Egypt. It also sees the constitution of the Jews as a uniquely holy people to be a part of this act of redemption. In October 1917 Buber wrote: "He who does not himself remember that God led him out of Egypt, he who does not himself await the Messiah, is no longer a true Jew." [8]

For Buber, Christianity always seemed to be a genuinely Jewish movement which was corrupted in its earliest beginnings by alien influences.[9]

In *Two Types of Faith*, Buber makes an intensive study of

the contrast between Jesus as seen in the synoptic Gospels and the teachings of Paul, the writer of John's Gospel, and others in the New Testament.

He attempts to show the reality of the Jewishness of Jesus, of his power to speak to Jews in a way that they could understand, a way in which a non-Jew could never speak. He makes no effort to disprove the teachings of Christianity; rather, he is concerned with comparing the New Testament to the Old Testament and to Pharisaic Judaism.

Buber's understanding of Jesus can only be seen within the context of his thought on messianism, especially as it involves the prophetic message to be found in Second Isaiah and the apocalyptic emphasis of the book of Daniel. In the earlier work, known as Deutero-Isaiah, we see the "servant" passages which refer to the prophets who proclaim the divine will even though it means suffering and death:

> The Lord called me from the womb
>   from the body of my mother he named my name.
> He made my mouth like a sharp sword,
>   in the shadow of his hand he hid me;
> he made me a polished arrow,
>   in his quiver he hid me away.
> And he said to me, "You are my servant,
>   Israel, in whom I will be glorified." [10]

None of these prophets ever claimed to be the messiah. Buber believes that Jesus worked and taught within the framework of this servant concept. It is his opinion that the life of Jesus cannot be understood if it is not recognized that Jesus must be considered in view of the "servant of the Lord" concept as it is found in Deutero-Isaiah. Even Albert Schweitzer has made this observation.[11]

Buber sees that Jewish teaching regarding the messiah is

not merely a belief in a "unique final event" and in a "unique human being" as the center of the event, but rather a series of events and a series of men who speak as prophets and as suffering "servants of the Lord" to succeeding generations.

The messianic mystery, according to Buber, is based on hiddenness, and those to whom it comes are men described in Isaiah 49:2: "He made me a polished arrow, in his quiver he hid me away." Those who are chosen to live this role must do it as servants of the Lord. Each may be the Promised One but they cannot disclose their messiahship, for self-disclosure would destroy their work. Their hiddenness is part of their work of suffering.

But Jesus emerged from the hiddenness of the quiver, Buber believes, and, having emerged, became not the messiah, but rather the initiator of a series of men who openly claimed messiahship for themselves. From the viewpoint of Judaism, Buber feels that Jesus acknowledged to his own soul and then openly proclaimed to others his own messiahship and thereby stepped out of the seclusion which is the real "messianic secret" of the servants of God. Even though he was the purest, the most rightful, and the one most endowed with real messianic power, he was still the first.[12]

It was at one significant point in his career, Buber feels, that Jesus became aware of himself as the long-awaited messiah.

> Now when Jesus came into the district of Caesarea Philippi, he asked his disciples, "Who do men say that the Son of man is?" And they said, "Some say John the Baptist, others say Elijah, and others Jeremiah or one of the prophets." He said to them, "But who do you say that I am?" Simon Peter replied, "You are the Christ, the Son of the living God." And Jesus answered him, "Blessed are you, Simon Bar-Jona! For flesh and blood has not revealed this to you, but my Father who is

in heaven." . . . Then he strictly charged the disciples to tell
no one that he was the Christ.[13]

Jesus steps out of the quiver and declares that he is the
messiah in a prophetic, servant-oriented sense. When he is
taken prisoner and brought to trial, Buber believes that Jesus
leaves the worldly prophetic servant tradition and enters into
the otherworld by the messianism found in the book of Daniel.[14]

> Now the chief priests and the whole council sought false testi-
> mony against Jesus that they might put him to death, but they
> found none, though many false witnesses came forward. At last
> two came forward and said, "This fellow said, 'I am able to de-
> stroy the temple of God, and to build it in three days.' " . . . But
> Jesus was silent. And the high priest said to him, "I adjure
> you by the living God, tell us if you are the Christ, the Son of
> God." Jesus said to him, "You have said so. But I tell you,
> hereafter you will see the Son of man seated at the right hand
> of Power, and coming on the clouds of heaven." Then the high
> priest tore his robes, and said, "He has uttered blasphemy." [15]

It is at this point that a gap is developed between Judaism
and Christianity which can never be bridged. Although Buber
views Jesus as a great man who played a definite role within
the history of Jewish messianism, he would have been num-
bered as a prophet in line with those who were servants of the
Lord, as indicated in Deutero-Isaiah, if he had not taken upon
himself the otherworldly messianism found in the Book of
Daniel.

Buber tries to show that in many ways the thinking of
Jesus is the same as the Jewish position. Jesus' attitude that
the commandments must be fulfilled is essentially the same
as the Jewish attitude, and both agree that the heart of man
is by nature without direction and "there is no direction except
to God." [16]

In the Sermon on the Mount, Jesus states: "Think not that I have come to abolish the law and the prophets; I have come not to abolish them but to fulfill them." [17] Buber sees this as agreeing with Pharisaic doctrine and bringing it to new heights. He feels that Jesus was attempting to make the Torah manifest in its original and full meaning and thereby bring it to life. Although the Sermon on the Mount appears at first glance to be at odds with the teachings of the Pharisees, in actual fact, "it is only the sublimation of a Pharisaic doctrine from a definite and fundamental point of view." [18]

Often the differences that existed between Jesus and the Pharisees were simply matters of degree and emphasis. Both stood within the same basic faith relationship to God. Jesus, however, made the divine demand more penetrating and incisive. "It becomes evident," Buber states, "that Jesus and central Pharisaism belong essentially to one another. . . ." [19]

It was Paul, Buber believes, who, in contrast to Jesus, turned away from the Old Testament conception of the kingship of God and the immediate relationship that is possible between God and man and instead developed a dualism between faith and action based on a belief that it was impossible for man to fulfill the law. Buber believes that it was "that gigantic figure, Paul, whom we must regard as the real originator of the Christian conception of faith." [20]

It is clear that Buber makes an unusual distinction between Judaism and Christianity. Jesus is seen as reflecting the prophets and the nonhypocritical wing of the Pharisees and is considered a part of classical Judaism. When Paul enters the Christian scene, a tremendous shift takes place. Jesus, Buber believes, had a direct relationship to God. With Paul a new emphasis is made: "I am the door; if any one enters by me, he will be saved." [21] Jesus believed in the immediacy of prayer,

Buber states, but with Paul it is as though a wall has been built around God and only one door can be opened to reach him. Only those who enter through this door will see the redeeming God. All others are left to the Satanic host.[22]

Paul believed that God created man as a creature with two warring natures. This was the basis of his dualism:

> We know that the law is spiritual; but I am carnal, sold under sin. I do not understand my own actions. For I do not do what I want, but I do the very thing I hate. Now if I do what I do not want, I agree that the law is good. So then it is no longer I that do it, but sin which dwells within me. For I know that nothing good dwells within me, that is, in my flesh. I can will what is right, but I cannot do it. For I do not do the good I want, but the evil I do not want is what I do. Now if I do what I do not want, it is no longer I that do it, but sin which dwells within me.
>
> So I find it to be a law that when I want to do right, evil lies close at hand. For I delight in the law of God, in my inmost self, but I see in my members another law at war with the law of my mind and making me captive to the law of sin which dwells in my members. Wretched man that I am! Who will deliver me from this body of death? Thanks be to God through Jesus Christ our Lord! [23]

Buber states that there are but two basic types of faith in life. In one, we trust someone without being able to give any sufficient reasons for trusting him; while in the other we acknowledge that a thing is true, also without being able to give any sufficient reasons for our belief. In the first instance faith begins when our entire being comes into contact with the one whom we trust. In the second instance, acknowledging that a thing is true depends on an act of acceptance by our entire being.

In the first relationship of faith a man "finds himself." In the second, he is "converted" to it. Buber believes that "the man who finds himself in it is primarily the member of a community whose covenant with the Unconditioned includes and determines him within it; the man who is converted to it is primarily an individual, one who has become an isolated individual, and the community arises as the joining together of the converted individuals." [24]

The first of these two types of faith is to be found in the early period of Israel; the second, in the early period of Christianity. It is this type of faith that Paul brings into existence. Buber insists that while, for Jesus, God could be known as a Father in an immediate relationship, for Paul, God becomes remote and removed from his people. God, for Paul, Buber says, uses men simply to bring about the fulfillment of the divine plan that he has established for the world. [25]

The most significant part of the plan as Paul sees it is that man is saved from his sin—the sin in his members over which he has no control—by Jesus Christ. Buber believes that Paul laid the foundation for the belief that Christ is a Person of the Godhead. Only God himself can bring about the propitiation of man's guilt, by having his Son, the Christ, suffer for the sake of others so that those who believe in him are saved by him. God the Father created a world in need of salvation and God the Son suffers in order to have the world. Buber feels that the prophetic concept that man must suffer for God's sake was changed by Paul so that God must suffer for man's sake. In this way Buber sees a new image of God being created which ultimately consoled and gave power to Christians for over a thousand years. [26]

All this causes Buber to conclude: "When I contemplate this God I no longer recognize the God of Jesus, nor his world, in this world of Paul's." [27] Buber feels that the faith of Jesus himself was clearly an example of complete trust in the person of the heavenly Father, while Paul's faith emphasizes belief in a risen Lord sitting at the right hand of God.[28] We go from the first of Buber's two types of faith to the second.

After Paul, others in the New Testament, specifically the writer of John's Gospel, continued the conversion of the Old Testament's trust in God into a belief that certain things were true about Jesus, his life, and his teachings. After the New Testament was complete, the work of Paul was carried to completion by Christian theologians until in A.D. 451, at the Council of Chalcedon, Jesus was recognized as the second person in the trinitarian Godhead, completely human and yet in an inexplicable way, completely divine.[29]

Max Brod, in his analysis of Judaism and Christianity in Buber's work, refers to Jesus' remarks: "Why do you call me good? No one is good but God alone." [30] He indicates that Buber believed that "no theological interpretation is able to weaken the directness of this assertion." The genuineness of the statements can hardly be doubted, especially since they were preserved in spite of the Christology that was developed by the early church. Buber, asserts Brod, saw in these remarks that Jesus was continuing the Old Testament proclamation of the nonhuman status of God and the nondivine status of man seen from his own personal points of reference. Jesus expected deification after his death, Buber believed, and his remarks seem to be resisting this development. He seems to be rejecting the idea of anyone's having faith in him and is instead favoring a direct faith in God which he wanted to help others to achieve.

But Brod also emphasizes that Buber did not overlook the "impressive historical fact" that because of their faith in Christ, a great salvation came to the Gentiles. Because they believed in Jesus as God, he "did not fail them in the hours when the world fell to pieces about them and . . . offered them atonement in the hours in which they found themselves fallen into guilt." Brod feels that Buber treats Christianity fairly, considering that it is not his own faith, and in Buber's judgment is also not the belief of Jesus.[31]

There are many other conclusions Buber reaches in regard to Christianity, but this, in broad strokes, is his major thought. Although we can say that his views on Jesus and Paul, and the influence of Pauline thinking on Christian theology, is based on a thorough, deeply investigated scholarship and must be recognized as valid since he is able to support his conclusions with biblical and nonbiblical evidence, we must add that Buber is also highly selective. In his examination of Jesus he chooses those teachings and experiences which reflect Jesus' Jewishness but ignores those teachings and beliefs which are similar to Paul's. Buber neglects the many places where Paul's position is almost identical to Jesus' in the synoptic Gospels. He chooses to omit a great deal in his reading of Paul. His thinking is valid as far as it goes, but it does not go far enough.

Also, his writing seems to imply that because the Christian faith has a belief that something is true, it is somehow less valid than a faith, such as Judaism, that has its basis in trust. This is a weakness in Buber's thinking. Can an ultimate distinction be made between these two types? Does one type of faith necessarily exclude the other? Not necessarily. It is difficult to accept the idea that just because a person believes something is true, that automatically excludes the possibility of a relationship of trust in God. On the contrary, the two types of faith must get together with each other. When one believes that something is true about Jesus, one also trusts in him and in God the Father. A person, and especially a Christian, cannot possibly have a real, living, dynamic faith without trust. Trust must always be at the heart of any relationship to God. Although that trust at times must be based on various uncertainties about God—since man is never able in his finiteness to understand the Infinite—he nevertheless is able to know God's trustworthiness from what he knows otherwise. Like the Jew, the Christian is able to determine in many ways the trustworthiness of God, but always if he has the eyes to see, he can depend on—and trust—God's working in human history.

Buber was never able to accept the Christian belief of Jesus as the divine Son of God. He spoke highly of him as an important member of the ancient Jewish community, and although he had a high regard for him, he could only see him as a man. He made this clear when he gave an address in Jerusalem commemorating his great Christian socialist friend, Leonhard Ragaz. His statement indicates where he believes Jesus fits into the Jewish community, and although sympathetic, he also reveals his Jewish beliefs:

> I firmly believe that the Jewish community, in the course of its renaissance, will recognize Jesus; and not merely as a great figure in its religious history, but also in the organic context of a Messianic development extending over millennia, whose final goal is the Redemption of Israel and of the world. But I believe equally firmly that we will never recognize Jesus as the Messiah Come, for this would contradict the deepest meaning of our Messianic passion. . . . There are no knots in the mighty cable of our Messianic belief which, fastened to a rock on Sinai, stretches to a still invisible peg anchored in the foundation of the world. In our view, redemption occurs forever, and none has yet occurred. Standing, bound and shackled, in the pillory of mankind, we demonstrate with the bloody body of our people the unredeemedness of the world. For us there is no cause of Jesus; only the cause of God exists for us.[32]

Buber observed that "to the Christian the Jew is the uncomprehensibly obdurate man, who declines to see what has happened; and to the Jew the Christian is the incomprehensibly daring man, who affirms in an unredeemed world that its redemption has been accomplished. This is a gulf which no human power can bridge."

But, having said that, it would be wrong and unfair to leave it there, because Buber had a deep compassion for men of other faiths and understood what Christianity was striving to accomplish. He made that clear when he wrote:

> It behooves both you and us to hold inviolably fast to our own true faith, that is, to our own deepest relationship to truth. It behooves both of us to show a religious respect for the true faith of the other. That is not what is called "tolerance"; our task is not to tolerate each other's waywardness, but to acknowledge the real relationship in which both stand to the truth. Whenever we both, Christian and Jew, care more for God Himself than for our images of God, we are united in the feeling that our Father's house is differently constructed than our human models take it to be.[33]

VIII. Interpreting Buber's Significance

There is little doubt that Martin Buber must be considered to be one of the great religious thinkers of this century. While he lived, he was easily the most influential Jewish theologian and philosopher of his day. Every other theologian and philosopher of importance in the Christian as well as the Jewish community was influenced by his thought. Not only was his thinking creative, it was also a clear call to mankind to fulfill its moral responsibilities. In this regard, he has often been linked with such men as Mahatma Gandhi and Albert Schweitzer. But his influence has gone far beyond philosophy and theology, especially his thinking regarding I-Thou. It has had a great impact in sociology, psychology, education, medicine, and political science.

Because it is not always easy to understand his thought, especially since those who first approach the task lack an understanding of the necessary background, Buber is often misunderstood and misinterpreted. It is hoped that the reader will find this introduction to Buber's life and thought sufficiently motivating so that he will want to delve into it much more deeply, recognizing that the profundity of the subject requires a serious approach and an earnest desire to discover the golden insights that await those who persevere. For they are there, but as with most things of value in this life, they appear only to those who are willing to accept the struggle.

To the serious student of Buber's thought, the German edition of his works, published in three large volumes between 1962 and 1964 and consisting of over 3,500 pages, is probably the most complete. There is nothing in English that approaches the completeness of the German work. The Hebrew Bible which he wrote in conjunction with Franz Rosenzweig is not included in the German volumes, but can be found separately. A number of editions in English are available.

When we look at Buber, we must realize that although he was born in the last quarter of the nineteenth century, he was always a man living in the modern world, the world of the present. He is still able to speak to us and suggest a way out of the predicaments and dilemmas men find themselves in today.

An extensive study could be made of the influence on his life of such men as the philosopher Friedrich Nietzsche, the novelist Feodor Dostoevsky and the theologian Sören Kierkegaard. But much of Buber's thought is unique. He was always open to new ideas and to the thinking of others, but in the final analysis he would accept or reject only that which added to his unique thought.

If we were to summarize his positive contributions, we would have to begin by saying that his greatest contribution must be his understanding of man and the human situation. In a world where man stands alone, a self-centered solitary figure, unable to reach out to other men and rarely to God, Buber attempted to indicate what man could and should be— a real person involved in real dialogue with his fellowman and with God.

It was through his understanding of the I-Thou and the I-It that Buber, over fifty years ago, was able to illuminate a new approach to life, the world, and other men: "All real living is meeting." All that Buber has to say always returns to this statement as the core of his thought. It is only when a man is truly able to confront another with openness, directness, and honesty; when he is able to trust and assume responsibility for another; when he meets another's Thou; only then does a man experience genuine humanity. Anything else would leave a man in the world of the It, and although he might find comfort and security, he would never truly know what it is to be a man, to be human.

Buber showed us that a man approaches all things in this world as either Thou or It, not just other men. Nature, art, literature, and all the spiritual creations of man open the world for him to real relation. Buber never condemned the world of I-It, because it was needed by science, and in most of what man did in life; but the I-Thou gave life its meaning.

Reinhold Niebuhr in America described the appearance of Buber's classic little book *I and Thou* as "a great event in the religious life of the West." In England, J. H. Oldham wrote: "I question whether any book has been published in the present century the message of which, if it were understood, would have such far-reaching consequence for the life of our time." And Emil Brunner in Switzerland has stated that Buber's discovery and development of the I-Thou and the I-It has brought about "a 'Copernican revolution' in the thinking not only of

Europe but of the whole of mankind." Buber's creative thought has called men to act with maturity and with moral responsibility.[1]

The second contribution that Buber has made is in his thought concerning God. He has shown an age that no longer centers its life in anything beyond itself that it is still possible to meet a living, personal God—the eternal Thou—in all the experiences of life. This God of the Hebrew Scriptures, the God of Abraham, Isaac, and Jacob, can be known as a living reality in every man's life. It is when we are able to meet the Thou in others that we begin to see what God is like. God can be seen and addressed through every Thou that we meet. Whenever we experience dialogue, God is present. Those who philosophize about God and discuss him, may point to God, but only those who, as persons, meet others in true encounter have any chance of ever meeting him.

How does one meet the eternal Thou? By opening himself up to relation with other human beings. Too often man builds a barrier of separation between himself and others. This happens when his life is lived on the level of I-It. God can never be possessed, but he can be met in dialogical relation.

Another major contribution made by Buber is his view of Scripture. He believed that his philosophy of dialogue was rooted in biblical faith. He saw the Hebrew Bible as a record of the actual meetings in history between God and Israel. The theme of Hebrew Scripture he saw as the encounter between God and his chosen people. It is both divine and human in the events it reports.

To Buber, the Bible is a document which proclaims that the world had a beginning and that it has a goal. Every generation is faced with accepting it as the true history of the world. But it can only do that when it approaches the Bible in the attitude of I-Thou. Only when a man is able to give himself totally to the Bible, without reservation, and with an openness to the possibility of faith, only then will he ever be able to understand its truths. Certainly, Buber's translation, with Franz Rosenzweig, of the Hebrew Bible into German must be acknowledged as a great achievement. Many consider it to be the best in existence.

Nahum N. Glatzer feels that Buber's translation of the Bible is an achievement which has taken away layers and layers of overgrowth from the ancient text. The most often quoted passages of Scripture have generally lost their original impact and freshness. The language of living words in the Bible has been replaced over the centuries by concepts abstracted from reality. When the important translations appeared, the Septuagint, the Vulgate, and Martin Luther's, their primary concern was to establish a valid testimonial for their respective communities, such as the early Church and the Reformation Church. There was little consideration given to preserving the original character of the Bible. Buber's work is seen as an attempt to rediscover the original writing.[2]

Buber had a deep understanding of the biblical way of speaking, and one of the most important features of his study of the Bible resulted from the way he used ancient Near Eastern materials better to understand the uniqueness of the Jewish faith. He often referred to Arabic, Accadian (Sumarian), Egyptian, and Canaanite literary practices and traditions in order better to comprehend particular passages. His primary concern, however, was always with an individual's existential encounter of the biblical event in the present moment.[3]

A fourth contribution, and one which has preserved for Western civilization a unique religious phenomenon, was

Buber's study of Hasidism and his gathering of Hasidic tales. Buber saw Hasidism as the most significant attempt since the time of the prophets at bringing into existence a true community based on religious principles. Here he saw men bound together in a spirit of brotherly love. It was from Hasidism that Buber developed much of his thought. He felt that through Hasidism the world of the everyday could be made holy; that the breach between God and the world could be bridged. He liked Hasidism's acceptance of the realities of life and felt that the joy that it expressed reflected the divine. It was a good life, he felt, regardless of all the evil, sin, and sorrow in the world. The message of Hasidism could make men free and lift them to a higher existence in their ordinary day-to-day experiences. It is well to recall Hermann Hesse's words again: "He [Buber] has enriched world literature with a genuine treasure as has no other living author—the Tales of the Hasidim. . . ."

As a fifth contribution we must recognize Buber's role as a theological bridge-builder. Although always Jewish, he was able to affect the thinking of countless Christian theologians and philosophers. By his insights he was able to help men of other religious traditions develop greater understanding of their own religious beliefs. His philosophy of dialogue, his concept of God as the eternal Thou, his understanding of Scripture were but a few areas which caused Christian thinkers to respect and study his thought. By making it easier for Christians to appreciate and love their Jewish brethren and influencing many in Judaism to see in Christianity those who were sincerely seeking meaning in life he added to the brotherhood of all men.

James Muilenburg, the great Old Testament scholar, felt that Buber was "the foremost Jewish speaker to the Chris-

tian community." He believed that Buber, more than any other
Jew, told the Christian what the words of the Old Testament
were really saying. For Muilenburg, Buber was "the great
Jewish teacher of Christians." He understood the New Testament and had a deep regard for the historical Jesus. He saw,
more than any other Jewish thinker, where the Jew and the
Christian parted and went their separate ways. As he gave
Jewish answers to Christian questions he helped the Christian
to understand himself.[4]

Finally, it has been said that example is an effective method
of teaching others; in fact, it is the best method. I believe I
must say that the example of Buber, the sincere, humble
teacher—his personality and his life—must also be seen as a
contribution that he has made. It is impossible to read his
works or to learn about him and not feel the impact of the
man. In a world that does not always believe in ideals and
principles, Martin Buber was one who never compromised his
beliefs. He was ready to speak out for whatever he felt was the
truth regardless of whether it was popular or not. The spirit
of his being, his warmth and basic humanity, were always
evident.

On his eighty-fifth birthday, in 1963, about three hundred
students from Hebrew University came to his home bearing
torches to pay him homage. As they filled his garden and
illuminated the darkness with the torches, he walked out onto
his veranda. He was constantly smiling, feeling a deep ap-
preciation for what was happening.

The students sang to him. Then as he spoke to them briefly,
all were silent. Afterwards he invited them into his home for
cookies and soft drinks.

Never a man of pretense, he was constantly concerned about
the needs of others. Along with his thought, the example of his

life and the depth of his personality—not unlike that of Albert
Schweitzer—will influence others for years to come.

Aubrey Hodes, in his excellent "intimate portrait" of
Buber, states that Buber was basically a teacher. For Hodes,
he was the greatest teacher of his generation. He never attempted to impose his own ideas on his pupils, but rather
asked questions which made them find their own answers. For
Buber education meant freedom, so he wanted his students to
go their own individual ways, even if they rebelled against
him. His idea of the correct way to teach was "the personal
example springing spontaneously and naturally from the whole
man." To Buber this meant a constant examination of one's
own conscience, for he believed that a teacher could not in-
struct others if he himself was flawed.[5]

It was only in his whole being, Buber believed, in all his
spontaneity, that a teacher could really affect the whole being
of the student. You did not need to be a moral genius, but you
did need to be a man who was completely alive and able to
communicate directly with others. It is when the teacher makes
no attempt at affecting others that his aliveness reaches them
and affects them most strongly and purely.[6]

How do we summarize and assess this unique human being?
What will he mean to future generations? For those who take
the time to study his thought, Buber will always offer the
truths of ancient faith as a remedy for the ills of modern man.
It is not possible to get lost in his thought and remain in an
ivory tower. Many theologians and philosophers offer us systems of thought which have little to do with the things we
feel and experiences we have in life. Their appeal is only to
the intellect. This is unacceptable to Buber. His emphasis is on
the everyday. His thinking deals with the real, the concrete,
and the particular. He goes deeper than speaking only to a

man's mind, reaching into his soul, his emotions, and into the wholeness of a man. Buber's struggle to meet the Thou in the world around him and thereby to meet the eternal Thou is everyman's struggle, whether we are aware of it or not.

Walter Kaufman has stated that Buber always strived to answer one central question: "What does the religion of my fathers mean to me today?" This question, of course, has been asked by many others, but very few have said so much of such importance in response to it. Buber has shown us what religion can be at its best. While he was not an authoritative spokesman for Judaism—that religious faith has no authoritative spokesmen—Buber did reveal a possible meaning for religion in a modern era full of criticism and irreligion.[7]

How does a man live in an unsaved world? Where does a man get the strength and the faith to live an ethical, just life in an often unethical and unjust world? Buber is able to point the way.

Notes

CHAPTER I

1. Paul Arthur Schilpp and Maurice Friedman, eds., *The Philosophy of Martin Buber*, pp. 3–4.
2. Martin Buber, *Hasidism and Modern Man*, p. 56.
3. Martin Buber, *Between Man and Man*, pp. 22–23.
4. Martin Buber, "My Road to Hasidism," *Memoirs of My People: Jewish Self-Portraits from the 11th to the 20th Centuries*, ed. Leo W. Schwarz (New York: Schocken Books, 1963), p. 515.
5. Ibid.
6. Buber, *Hasidism and Modern Man*, p. 56.
7. Martin Buber, *The Prophetic Faith*, p. 46.
8. From a letter of Hesse to a friend explaining his nomination of Buber for a Nobel Prize in literature in 1949. Quoted in Maurice S. Friedman, *Martin Buber: The Life of Dialogue*, p. 6.
9. Friedman, *Martin Buber: The Life of Dialogue*, p. 27.
10. Malcolm L. Diamond, *Martin Buber: Jewish Existentialist*, p. 7.
11. Ibid., p. 11.
12. Martin Buber, *I and Thou*, pp. 87–88.
13. Quoted by Aubrey Hodes, *Martin Buber: An Intimate Portrait*, p. 52.
14. Schilpp and Friedman, *The Philosophy of Martin Buber*, pp. 25–26.
15. Ibid., pp. 381–82.

16. Buber, *I and Thou,* trans. Ronald Gregor Smith (Edinburgh: T. & T. Clark, 1937), p. 11.

17. Roy Oliver, *The Wanderer and the Way,* p. 8.

18. Buber, *Between Man and Man,* p. 15.

19. Martin Buber, *Israel and the World,* pp. 176–77.

20. Ibid., pp. 173–82.

21. Friedman, *Martin Buber: The Life of Dialogue,* pp. 110–11.

22. Schilpp and Friedman, *The Philosophy of Martin Buber,* pp. 725–26.

23. Diamond, *Martin Buber: Jewish Existentialist,* p. 208.

24. Martin Buber, *At the Turning: Three Addresses on Judaism,* p. 61.

25. Martin Buber, *Two Types of Faith,* p. 168.

26. Buber, *The Prophetic Faith,* p. 183.

27. Martin Buber, *Pointing the Way,* p. 232.

28. Ibid., p. 233.

29. Ibid., pp. 236–37.

30. Ibid., p. 239.

31. Martin Buber, *A Believing Humanism,* pp. 57–59.

32. Ibid., pp. 57–58.

33. Buber's address is entitled "Hope for This Hour" and can be found in *Pointing the Way,* p. 220.

34. Henry P. van Dusen, *Dag Hammarskjöld: The Statesman and His Faith* (New York: Harper and Row, 1966), p. 187.

35. Buber, *A Believing Humanism,* p. 58.

36. Dag Hammarskjöld, *Markings,* trans. Leif Sjoberg (New York: Alfred A. Knopf, 1964), p. 85.

37. Van Dusen, *Dag Hammarskjöld,* p. 187.

38. Hodes, *Martin Buber: An Intimate Portrait,* p. 146. The basic thread of the story of Buber's relationship to Dag Hammarskjöld was obtained from this excellent study of Buber by Mr. Hodes.

39. Buber, *A Believing Humanism,* p. 229.

40. Editorial, *New York Times,* June 14, 1965, p. 32.

CHAPTER II

1. Buber, *I and Thou,* 2nd ed., p. 11.

2. Ibid., p. 3.

3. Ibid., pp. 12–13.

4. Ibid., p. 11.

5. Ibid., p. 102.

6. Ibid., p. 34.
7. Ibid., p. 15.
8. Ibid., pp. 14–15.
9. Ibid., p. 16.
10. Hodes, *Martin Buber: An Intimate Portrait*, p. 56.
11. Buber, *Between Man and Man*, p. 184.
12. Martin Buber, *Der heilige Weg: Eine Antwort an die Juden und die Völker.* Quoted by Will Hesberg in *The Writings of Martin Buber* (New York: Meridian Books, 1956), p. 19.
13. Buber, *I and Thou*, p. 106.
14. Hodes, *Martin Buber: An Intimate Portrait*, p. 57.
15. Martin Buber, "The Question of the Single One," *Israel and the World: Essays in a Time of Crisis*, p. 71.

CHAPTER III

1. Buber, "Postscript," *I and Thou*, pp. 123–24.
2. Ibid., p. 75.
3. Martin Buber, *Eclipse of God: Studies in the Relation between Religion and Philosophy*, pp. 15–18.
4. Ibid., pp. 76–79.
5. Ibid., p. 79.
6. Ibid., pp. 81–83.
7. Ibid., p. 89.
8. Ibid., pp. 87–88.
9. Ibid., p. 95.
10. Ibid., p. 98.
11. Ibid., pp. 98–99.
12. Ibid., p. 100.
13. Ibid.
14. Ibid., p. 101.
15. Ibid., p. 103.
16. Ibid., pp. 103–4.
17. Ibid., p. 105.
18. Ibid., p. 106.
19. Ibid., pp. 106–7.
20. Ibid., p. 109.
21. Ibid., p. 112.
22. Ibid., pp. 115–16.
23. Ibid., pp. 117–20.

CHAPTER IV

1. Martin Buber, *Hasidism,* p. 4.
2. Gershom G. Scholem, *Major Trends in Jewish Mysticism* (New York: Schocken Books, 1946), Eighth Lecture. This author has also written the finest single work on Sabbatai Sevi and the Sabbatian Movement during his lifetime: *Sabbatai Sevi: The Mystical Messiah, 1626–1676* (Princeton, N.J.: Princeton University Press, 1973).
3. Buber, *Hasidism,* p. 23.
4. Ibid., pp. 23–24.
5. Martin Buber, *To Hallow This Life,* p. 87.
6. Martin Buber, *Tales of the Hasidim: The Later Masters,* p. 87.
7. Martin Buber, *The Way of Man,* pp. 5–6.
8. Ibid., pp. 35–37.
9. Martin Buber, *Tales of the Hasidim: The Early Masters,* p. 240.
10. Ibid., p. 72.
11. Buber, *Tales of the Hasidim: The Later Masters,* p. 92.
12. Ibid., p. 208.
13. Ibid., p. 257.
14. Buber, *Tales of the Hasidim: The Early Masters,* p. 245.

CHAPTER V

1. Martin Buber, "The Man of Today and the Jewish Bible," *On the Bible,* p. 1.
2. Ibid., p. 2.
3. Ibid.
4. Ibid.
5. Ibid., pp. 3–4.
6. Ibid., p. 4.
7. Ibid., p. 5.
8. Ibid.
9. Ibid.
10. Ibid., p. 6.
11. Ibid., pp. 6–7.
12. Ibid., p. 8.
13. Ibid., pp. 8–9.
14. Ibid., pp. 9–10.
15. Ibid., pp. 10–11.
16. Ibid., pp. 11–12.

17. Ibid., p. 12.
18. Ibid., pp. 12–13.
19. Ibid., p. 13.

CHAPTER VI

1. Friedman, *Martin Buber: The Life of Dialogue*, p. 258.
2. Diamond, *Martin Buber: Jewish Existentialist*, pp. 148–49.
3. Buber, *Israel and the World*, pp. 158–59.
4. Buber, *Pointing the Way*, pp. 142–43.
5. Buber, *Israel and the World*, pp. 229–30.
6. Martin Buber, *On Judaism*, pp. 112–13.
7. Buber, *Israel and the World*, p. 232.
8. Buber, *On Judaism*, p. 116.
9. Buber, *Israel and the World*, p. 233.
10. Ibid.
11. Quoted by Aubrey Hodes in *Martin Buber: An Intimate Portrait*, p. 92.
12. Ibid., p. 99.
13. Ibid., p. 101.

CHAPTER VII

1. Joseph Houldsworth Oldham, *Real Life Is Meeting* (New York: Macmillan, 1947), pp. 13–16.
2. Paul Tillich, "Martin Buber and Christian Thought," *Commentary* 5, no. 6 (June 1948) : 397.
3. Hodes, *Martin Buber: An Intimate Portrait*, p. 184.
4. Schilpp and Friedman, *The Philosophy of Martin Buber*, p. 312.
5. Buber, *Two Types of Faith*, trans. Norman P. Goldhawk, p. 12 f.
6. Will Herberg, ed., *The Writings of Martin Buber*, pp. 29–30.
7. Rev. 22:20.
8. Herberg, *The Writings of Martin Buber*, p. 31.
9. Ibid., p. 37.
10. Isa. 49:1–3, RSV. Although Buber did not use this version, I have used it because it is better understood by the modern reader. Buber never refers to an Old Testament or a New Testament except in a work such as *Two Types of Faith*, where he is making a com-

parison of the two. Ordinarily, he would refer to the Old Testament as the Hebrew Bible, or the Jewish Bible.

11. Martin Buber, *For the Sake of Heaven*, p. xiii.
12. Buber, *Hasidism*, pp. 112–14.
13. Matt. 16:13–17, 20, RSV.
14. Buber, *Two Types of Faith*, pp. 106 ff.
15. Matt. 26:59–65, RSV.
16. Buber, *Two Types of Faith*, p. 63.
17. Matt. 5:17.
18. Buber, *Two Types of Faith*, pp. 62–63.
19. Ibid., p. 11.
20. Ibid., p. 44.
21. John 10:9.
22. Schilpp and Friedman, *The Philosophy of Martin Buber*, p. 329.
23. Rom. 7:14–25, RSV.
24. Schilpp and Friedman, *The Philosophy of Martin Buber*, pp. 7–9.
25. Ibid., p. 86.
26. Ibid., pp. 149–50.
27. Ibid., p. 89.
28. Ibid., pp. 10 f., 46 f.
29. Ibid., pp. 30–35, 102–116, 127–34.
30. Mark 10:18.
31. Schilpp and Friedman, *The Philosophy of Martin Buber*, pp. 332–33.
32. Quoted in Ernst Simon, "Martin Buber: His Way between Thought and Deed," *Jewish Frontier* 15 (February 1948) : 26.
33. Buber, *Israel and the World*, pp. 39–40.

CHAPTER VIII

1. Bernard Martin, ed., *Great Twentieth Century Jewish Philosophers*, p. 238.
2. Schilpp and Friedman, *The Philosophy of Martin Buber*. p. 364.
3. Ibid., pp. 381–82.
4. Ibid., p. 382.
5. Hodes, *Martin Buber: An Intimate Portrait*, p. 118.
6. Buber, *Between Man and Man*, p. 105.
7. Schilpp and Friedman, *The Philosophy of Martin Buber*, p. 666.

Selected Bibliography

This bibliography is a brief listing of some of the more important works written by or about Martin Buber and available in English.

I. WORKS BY MARTIN BUBER

Am v'Olam. Jerusalem: Zionist Library, 1961.

At the Turning: Three Addresses on Judaism. New York: Farrar, Straus and Young, 1952.

A Believing Humanism: My Testament 1902–1965. Translated by Maurice S. Friedman. New York: Simon and Schuster, 1967.

Between Man and Man. Translated by Ronald Gregor Smith. London: Routledge and Kegan Paul, 1947. New York: Macmillan, 1948.

Daniel: Dialogues on Realization. Translated by Maurice S. Friedman. New York: Holt, Rinehart and Winston, 1964; McGraw-Hill paperback edition, 1965.

Eclipse of God: Studies in the Relation between Religion and Philosophy. Translated by Maurice S. Friedman. New York: Harper and Brothers, 1952; Harper and Row Torchbook edition, 1957.

For the Sake of Heaven: A Chronicle. Translated by Ludwig Lewisohn. Philadelphia: Jewish Publication Society, 1945. New York: Harper and Brothers, 1953; Atheneum paper edition, 1969.

Good and Evil: Two Interpretations. New York: Charles Scribner's Sons, 1953.

Hasidism. Translated by Greta Hort. New York: Philosophical Library, 1948.

Hasidism and Modern Man. Edited and translated by Maurice S. Friedman. New York: Horizon Press, 1958; Harper and Row Torchbook edition, 1966.

I and Thou. Translated by Ronald Gregor Smith. New York: Charles Scribner's Sons, 1937, 1958. Translated by Walter Kaufman. New York: Charles Scribner's Sons, 1970.

Israel and Palestine: The History of an Idea. Translated by Stanley Godman. London: East and West Library, 1952. New York: Farrar, Straus and Young, 1952.

Israel and the World: Essays in a Time of Crisis. Translated by Olga Marx and others. New York: Schocken Books, 1948, 1963.

Jewish Mysticism and the Legends of the Baalshem. Translated by Lucy Cohen. London: J.M. Dent and Sons Ltd., 1931.

Kingship of God. Translated by Richard Scheimann. New York: Harper and Row, 1967.

The Knowledge of Man. Edited by Maurice S. Friedman. Translated by Maurice S. Friedman and Ronald Gregor Smith. London: Allen and Unwin, 1965. New York: Harper and Row, 1966.

The Legend of the Baal-Shem. Translated by Maurice S. Friedman. New York: Harper and Brothers, 1955.

Mamre: Essays in Religion. Translated by Greta Hort. Melbourne: Melbourne University Press, 1946.

Meetings. Edited by Maurice Friedman. LaSalle, Ill.: Open Court Publishing Company, 1973.

Moses: Revelation and the Covenant. Oxford: East and West Library, 1946. New York: Harper and Row Torchbook edition, 1958.

On Judaism. Edited by Nahum N. Glatzer. New York: Schocken Books, 1967.

On the Bible: Eighteen Studies. Edited by Nahum N. Glatzer. New York: Schocken Books, 1968.

Origin and Meaning of Hasidism. Translated by Maurice S. Friedman. New York: Horizon Press, 1960; Harper and Row Torchbook edition, 1966.

Paths in Utopia. Translated by R. F. C. Hull. London: Routledge and Kegan Paul, 1948. Boston: Beacon Press, 1958.

P'gishot. Jerusalem: Mosad Bialik, 1965.

Pointing the Way: Collected Essays. Translated by Maurice S. Friedman. New York: Harper and Brothers, 1957; Harper and Row Torchbook edition, 1963.

The Prophetic Faith. Translated by Carlyle Witton-Davies. New York: Macmillan, 1949; Harper and Row Torchbook edition, 1960.

Right and Wrong: An Interpretation of Some Psalms. Translated by Ronald Gregor Smith. London: SCM Press, 1952.

Tales of the Hasidim: The Early Masters. Translated by Olga Marx. New York: Schocken Books, 1947.

Tales of the Hasidim: The Later Masters. Translated by Olga Marx. New York: Schocken Books, 1948.

Tales of Rabbi Nachman. Translated by Maurice S. Friedman. Bloomington, Ind.: Indiana University Press, 1962. New York: Horizon Press, 1968.

Ten Rungs: Hasidic Sayings. Translated by Olga Marx. New York: Schocken Books, 1947, 1962.

To Hallow This Life. Edited by Jacob Trapp. New York: Harper and Brothers, 1958.

Two Letters to Gandhi. With Judah Magnes. Jerusalem: Rubin Mass, 1939.

Two Types of Faith. Translated by Norman P. Goldhawk. London: Routledge and Kegan Paul, 1951. New York: Macmillan, 1952; Harper and Row Torchbook edition, 1961.

The Way of Man, According to the Teachings of Hasidism. London: Routledge and Kegan Paul, 1950. Chicago: Wilcox and Follett Co., 1951. New York: Citadel Press, 1966.

The Way of Response. Edited by Nahum N. Glatzer. New York: Schocken Books, 1966.

The Writings of Martin Buber. Edited by Will Herberg. New York: Meridian Books, 1956.

II. WORKS ABOUT MARTIN BUBER

Agus, Jacob B., *Modern Philosophies of Judaism.* New York: Behrman's Jewish Book House, 1941.

Balthasar, Hans Urs von, *Martin Buber and Christianity: A Dialogue between Israel and the Church.* Translated by Alexander Dru. New York: Macmillan, 1962.

Beek, Martinus A., and J. Sperna Weiland, *Martin Buber: Personalist and Prophet.* Paramus, N.J.: Paulist/Newman, 1968.

Bergman, Samuel Hugo, *Faith and Reason: An Introduction to Modern Jewish Thought.* Translated and edited by Alfred Jospe. New York: Schocken Books, 1961.

Cohen, Arthur A., *Martin Buber.* New York: Hillary House, 1957. London: Bowes and Bowes, 1957.

Diamond, Malcolm L., *Martin Buber: Jewish Existentialist.* New York: Oxford University Press, 1960; Harper and Row Torchbook edition, 1968.

Friedman, Maurice S., *Martin Buber: The Life of Dialogue.* Chicago: University of Chicago Press, 1955. New York: Harper and Row Torchbook edition, 1960.

Hodes, Aubrey, *Martin Buber: An Intimate Portrait.* New York: Viking Press, 1971.

Manheim, Werner, *Martin Buber.* New York: Twayne Publishers, Inc., 1974.

Martin, Bernard, ed., *Great Twentieth Century Philosophers.* London: Macmillan, 1970.

Oliver, Roy, *The Wanderer and the Way: The Hebrew Tradition in the Writings of Martin Buber.* Ithaca, N.Y.: Cornell University Press, 1968.

Pfuetze, Paul E., *The Social Self.* New York: Bookman Associates, 1954.

Schaeder, Grete, *The Hebrew Humanism of Martin Buber.* Translated by Noah J. Jacobs. Detroit: Wayne State University Press, 1973.

Schilpp, Paul A., and Maurice S. Friedman, eds., *Philosophy of Martin Buber.* LaSalle, Ill.: Open Court, 1967.

Smith, Ronald Gregor, *Martin Buber.* Richmond, Va.: John Knox Press, 1967.